P9-ASA-213
GOD MADE ME DO IT
TRUE STORIES of the worst ADVICE THE LORD HAS EVER GIVEN His FOLLOWERS
Marc Hartzman

sourcebooks

Published by Sourcebooks, Inc.
P.O. Box 4410, Naperville, Illinois 60567-4410
(630) 961-3900
Fax: (630) 961-2168
www.sourcebooks.com

Library of Congress Cataloging-in-Publication Data

Hartzman, Marc.
God made me do it : true stories of the worst advice the Lord has ever given his followers / Marc Hartzman.
p. cm.
1. God—Humor. 2. Religious adherents—Humor. I. Title.
PN6231.R4H37 2010
818'.602--dc22
2009039306

Printed and bound in the United States of America.
VP 10 9 8 7 6 5 4 3 2 1

For Lela and Scarlett

God, you've said some wacky things, but you've been good to me.

ACKNOWLEDGMENTS

In the tradition of many of the world's greatest athletes, I have to thank God, first and foremost, for making this book possible. He gave us life and some very interesting ways to live it. Now, on to the mortals: Katie Boyle, my agent, whose excitement from the beginning of this project put the wheels in motion and whose advice along the way kept it well on track; Peter Lynch, my editor, who listened to the Lord when He told him to publish this book, thank you for all your wonderful enthusiasm, guidance, and helpful suggestions; Brenda Horrigan, my copyeditor, Chris Stolle, my proofreader, and Anne Hartman, whose omniscience gave polish to my text and simply made this a better book; Kelly Bale for her work in securing all the images; Harrod Blank, Theresa Zelasko, Tammy Cromer-Campbell, Sam and Bonnie Steger for their photography contributions; Aric Cheston, Jon Cochran, Erik Contzius, Paul and Beverly Hartzman, Peter Mendez, Anthony Monahan, Maggie Morris, Greg Valvano, and Buck Wolf for their help and support; Mom and Dad for introducing me to God with a snip on my eighth day of life; Lela and Scarlett for being the two best girls a daddy could ever hope for; and finally, my wonderful wife Liz for her photography and her patience, support, and love.

OPENING SERMON

It is my profound honor to offer this book to you, the reader, and esteemed brethren everywhere. For it was I who was chosen to deliver it, not any one of the other several billion people milling about this wondrous planet. Whether it was through the greatest eenie-meenie-miny-moe the world has ever known or a well-informed divine decision, the Lord tapped me for this book.

It all began one partly cloudy evening when a healthy patch of shrubbery spontaneously burst into flames in my vicinity. I instinctively began to run from it, fearing for my own safety, but as I took that first step, I heard a deep, booming voice call my name. I immediately knew it wasn't James Earl Jones; we'd never met and he, too, would've fled from the horrific inferno.

It was God.

There He stood aglow, majestically adorned in a freshly ironed white tunic with His wavy, snowlike hair and long, flowing beard fluttering in a glorious breeze. The accuracy of God's numerous portrait artists over the years was simply uncanny.

With the heat blazing in my face, I dripped in sweat as God and I began our chat:

GOD: *Marc, I am the Lord your God, and I command thee to write a book! A book documenting my more recent conversations with my children of the world—my political leaders, my overpaid athletes, my murderers, my preachers, my bumpkins, and whoever else's ears I've whispered into. Spread the Lord's lesser-known and most outlandish words unto all who will listen.*

MH: *Is this burning bush really necessary? You know arson is illegal. We've come a long way since Moses.*

GOD: *This is exactly the point this book needs to make. Listen carefully, little man: Almighty as I am, supreme as I may be, I screw up now and then. I've got 6,706,993,152 people to look after and even more prayers to listen to. I've got heaven to manage, new creations to ponder, and that pesky Satan to thwart. I'm busy as hell. So sometimes, every here and there, I say things that might be regrettable.*

MH: *So you're making excuses?*

GOD: *Do you have any idea what a typical Sunday is like? Congregations from every corner of the Earth talking at once, starving people across the continents begging me for food, shouts from every hospital sick bed, and millions of fist-pumping shmohawks yammering on about their football team needing to win. And what makes you people* *think Earth is the only planet I'm in charge of? I'm a tug-of-war being yanked from infinite ends.*

MH: *But you're omnipotent. And, I might add, omnipresent.*

GOD: *I'm exactly what people define me as. Right now, I'm what you want me to be. In fact, are you really sure I'm even talking to you? Will anyone believe you? What will you say when the fire department arrives and you're charged with second-degree arson? You can speak to me every day, and no one will question you. But the moment you let someone know I answered, someone will offer you medication and an insulting smirk. Everyone wants to think an all-powerful being can't speak. Now, skedaddle—I hear sirens. Write the book, sell a million copies, and buy yourself something nice. Like I said, I command thee. And now I must go; there are sneezes I need to bless. Toodles!*

MH: *Wait! Quick question—if you created everything, who created you? Who?!?*

GOD: *[Drifting toward the heavens, offering a thumbs-up]*

MH: *Goddamn it!*

This book is my response to that remarkable conversation. Carrying out God's will took me on a wondrous journey through the past hundred-plus years. I scoured newspaper archives, dug through the vast information landfill of the Internet, combed through photo collections, visited and called local libraries, chatted with a documentary filmmaker and a "weird news" specialist, and climbed Mount Sinai a couple times.

With my mission accomplished and this book in your hands, you will see that God sometimes works in very mysterious and unpleasant ways. You'll find that He is excessively in the details, busying Himself with such tasks as perfecting caramel corn recipes and managing minor league baseball games. And you'll discover why things like world hunger have been on the Lord's back burner.

Of course, there are those who simply throw God under the bus as their handy scapegoat and then there are those who just aren't playing with a full deck or even a single card. As a result, the phrase "God told me to" has become the world's most overused and worst excuse for poor judgment, horrendous acts, and pure nonsense. It's a phrase that's dictated presidential policies, led to the murder of loved ones, set off deadly hunger strikes, encouraged cannibalism, provoked self-mutilation, caused the exhuming of corpses, spawned community relocations, and, for those who've heard all the aforementioned and more, led to the belief that there's no reason to believe. While God's words—or at least the idea of His words—has certainly helped and inspired many, as these pages will sometimes show, the world would be a better place if the Lord kept His words to Himself.

You may be thinking, it wasn't God who spoke to you, Marc. It was the devil, that sneaky Prince of Darkness. But if God can speak to Pat Robertson, George W. Bush, Joe Football Player, and countless evangelists, why not me or anyone else in this book? No one blames bad advice from those mentioned above on ol' Scratch.

For those who believed God really spoke to them, well, maybe He did. Maybe the Lord really did speak the words featured in this book. Maybe what He said about the occasional goof-up is spot-on: He's not perfect. And what that means is that maybe, just maybe, we truly are created in His image.

God bless,
Marc Hartzman

TRAFFIC ENLIGHTENMENT

"God told her to [direct traffic topless]."

Police report documenting the arrest of a thirty-year-old Florida woman, 2008

It was seven o'clock in the evening when a topless woman suddenly appeared in a central Florida intersection. She got motorists' attention for obvious reasons but created an even bigger spectacle by running in and out of the street as she attempted to direct traffic.

When police arrived on the scene, she was talking to herself in the middle of the road and began foaming at the mouth as she explained her holy mission. The officers promptly vetoed the Lord's directive and took the self-appointed traffic director to a mental facility. They also gave her a shirt.

ZOMBIE PRAYERS

"God said she will come back from the dead and that is what I believe."

Michael, on why he and his wife refused to bury their daughter for more than ten weeks, 1983

In 1983, Faith died as a result of complications from juvenile diabetes. The body of the ten-year-old was hidden in a sealed room inside the building housing her father's construction business for nearly three months. There, the family and a small religious group prayed mightily for her return as the corpse decomposed.

When a concerned member of the prayer group decided to tip off authorities, a judge ordered the body to be buried in order to meet county health laws. The family's minister agreed with the decision, claiming they should not have postponed laying Faith to rest while they waited for God to make good on His word. The girl's unwavering parents held fast to their beliefs and boycotted the burial.

God could have at least recommended cryogenics until He got around to the resurrection.

AN OFFICER AND A DEITY

"God told me to [back into Jesus's patrol car]."

Unidentified man responding to the police officer's question: "Dude, why did you hit me?" 2006

For no other reason than God's say-so, the thirty-year-old driver threw his 1983 Chevy pickup into reverse and smacked it into the cruiser belonging to a deputy named Jesus. Officer Jesus did not find it funny.

The damage to the vehicle was estimated at $3,900. And the man—not the Lord, who told him to do it—was charged with first-degree malicious mischief.

UNHEAVENLY HOME

"I got tired of always finding the sink full of dirty dishes. God told me to shoot her; I heard Him."

Hubert, on his reason for killing his wife, 1933

Hubert's wife had been found dead in his car the previous summer. He initially claimed robbers had shot her, but apparently he grew tired of doing his own dishes and eventually confessed.

On trial for first-degree murder, the thirty-two-year-old Illinois schoolteacher described his wife to jurors as slovenly, complaining she was more interested in her career than in homemaking. As a result, he explained, their home was a mess, and he was embarrassed to host friends and family.

The jury took less than twenty-four hours to arrive at a guilty verdict. Hubert was sentenced to death in the electric chair.

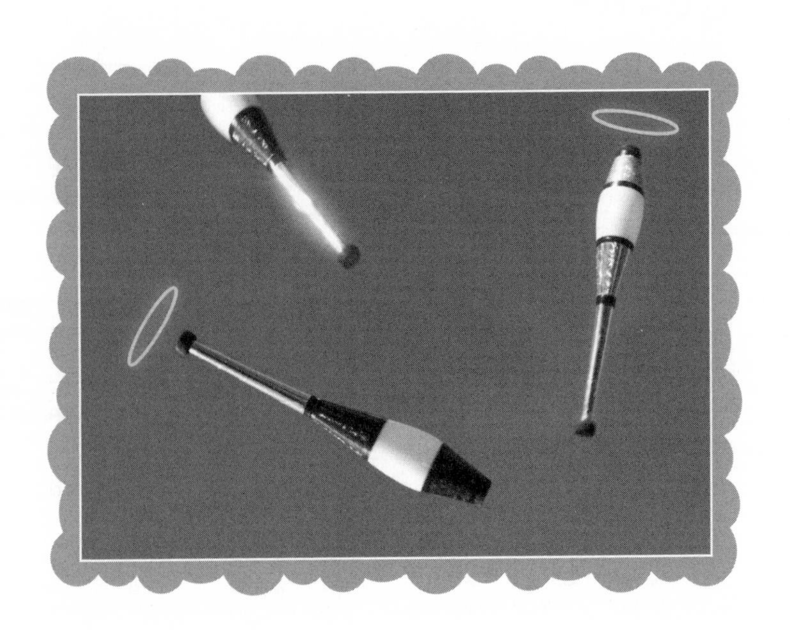

BUSKER MIRACLES

"God told me to come and juggle."

Nathan, juggling evangelist, on his 480-mile journey to Terri Schiavo's Florida hospice, 2005

When Terri Schiavo's feeding tube was removed under a controversial court order, protestors gathered outside the hospice and a full-fledged media circus ensued. Adding to the circus was Nathan, accompanied by his pregnant wife and two children, who juggled clubs while wearing a bright smile and an even brighter fluorescent orange tie.

Nathan believed that if it were God's desire, He could make Schiavo get up and walk again. Yet, she had spent fifteen years in a vegetative state, so if God had wanted to heal her, He wasn't having any luck. And, apparently, sending a juggler didn't do the trick either.

WORDS FROM WAY ABOVE

"I felt an overwhelming holy presence all around me. When I opened my eyes, there He stood…some 900 feet tall, looking at me…He stared at me without saying a word. Oh, I will never forget those eyes. He reached down his hands under the City of Faith, lifted it, and said to me, 'See how easy it is for me to lift it.'"

Oral Roberts, televangelist and university founder, in a fundraising letter regarding his vision of a supersized Jesus, 1980

Roberts and God are longtime associates, dating back to the early '60s when He instructed the televangelist to build Oral Roberts University in Tulsa, Oklahoma. Despite their established relationship, it wasn't until 1977 that Roberts had his first encounter with the gigantic Jesus, who instructed him to build a similarly massive hospital to be called the City of Faith Medical and Research Center.

It was just a few years later when Roberts wrote the letter on the previous page, encouraged by the 900-footer, to solicit more money from donors and to carry on with the construction.

"If you will obey," Roberts added in his letter, "it will not be difficult to finish the second half of the City of Faith."

The medical complex opened in 1981, adjacent to Roberts's university, and featured a sixty-story clinic, a thirty-story hospital, and a twenty-story research center.

Roberts's Jesus sighting remains the largest to date.

NEAR-DEATH EXPERIENCE

"If you don't [raise $8 million] then your work is finished, and I'm going to call you home."

Oral Roberts, telling his television audience how the Lord threatened his life if he didn't pull the City of Faith out of debt, 1987

It was March 1986 when God interrupted Roberts as he sat reading a spy novel and threatened his life. If the evangelist couldn't raise the money to keep the hospital running within a year, his next conversation with God would be in person. "He really spooked me," Roberts said. "He had my attention, believe me." So much for finishing that book.

By January 1987, Roberts had raised $3.5 million, but he needed to use his television platform to reach out and gather the remaining funds. He spent the first three months of 1987 praying, fasting, and waiting for money to roll in before the Lord's March 31 deadline. Amazingly, it did. Roberts hauled in more than $9 million just in time, with the last $1.3 million coming from a dog track owner.

Yet, even a fundraising miracle couldn't save the City

of Faith. By 1989, the seldom-used hospital closed at God's request and was eventually turned into an office building.

When Roberts asked the Lord why He wanted the facility to be shut down, He gave this response: "The mission has been accomplished in the same way that after the three years of public ministry My Son said on the cross, 'Father, it is finished.'"

So according to Roberts, in God's eyes this mighty feat of fundraising and construction was on equal footing with Jesus's entire public ministry.

PROFESSIONAL APOCALYPSE

"God told me to resign."

Richard Roberts, president of Oral Roberts University, after facing a lawsuit alleging lavish spending while the school struggled with a $50 million debt, 2007

As the school faced a massive debt, Roberts, the son of university founder Oral, allegedly went on a $39,000 shopping spree for his wife, bought a stable of horses for his children, and sent his daughter on a $29,000 senior trip to the Bahamas on the university's jet.

Roberts initially did not want to resign or give in to the lawsuit, and he claimed God had previously agreed with him. According to the big spender, the Lord originally told him, "We live in a litigious society. Anyone can get mad and file a lawsuit against another person whether they have a legitimate case or not. This lawsuit...is about intimidation, blackmail, and extortion." Apparently, God saw the light and decided a resignation was the more righteous move.

The Lord also promised Roberts that if he stepped down, the school would be blessed "supernaturally." Three days after the resignation, a wealthy businessman promised to help the school with a $70 million pledge.

SERPENT'S SANCTUARY

"I seen that big copperhead in there bite, but I know one thing: That the Lord told me it was all right. The Lord said it would be all right."

John, aka "Punkin," serpent-handling evangelist, just before being bitten and dying right before his congregation, 1998

Amidst a clapping and shouting congregation, John tried to cling to life after the serpent sunk its fang into the base of his middle finger. He'd been bitten more than twenty times in eighteen years of handling snakes. As he began to lose this most recent battle, a man screamed, "Right now, God! Help my brother right now! I'll glorify you. I'll praise you for it." God didn't help. John was dead within fifteen minutes.

The evangelist left behind five children. His wife had died three years earlier, also from a snakebite. Custody was split between the grandparents, but the paternal side had their own separate snake-handling church. The judge gave a specific order that the children were not to be taken to the church, but it was violated almost immediately. The Lord must have told them it was all right.

30,000 MILES CLOSER TO GOD

"The Lord spoke to me and said, 'You believe for a Citation 10 right now'...Father we receive it. We receive it as a gift from on high. It will never, ever be used for anything other than what is becoming to you Lord Jesus."

Kenneth Copeland, television evangelist, on presenting his new $20 million private jet to his congregants, 2007

Copeland, who heads the Believers Voice of Victory ministry and preaches prosperity, had congregants purchase the plane to help him spread his message around the globe. Uses "becoming to Lord Jesus" included alleged trips to a Colorado ski resort, a hunting expedition to kill God's creatures, and stopovers in Maui, Honolulu, and the Fiji Islands.

U.S. Senator Charles Grassley, a Republican member of the Senate Finance Committee, has investigated excessive spending by television evangelists like Copeland. He's targeted the preacher to find out if such private trips were reimbursed, but Copeland has remained defiant, refusing to submit any private financial records to Washington and telling his congregation, "Now you can go get a subpoena and I won't give it to you. It's not yours. It's God's! And you're not gonna get it. And that is something I'll go to prison over. So just get over it!"

Senator Grassley has yet to reveal any violations. Which means the government's not gonna get the enormous mansion Copeland's followers bought him and God either.

OUR FATHER, OUR DINNER

"We knew we had to eat [my father-in-law] and we did. I want it known we weren't ashamed. God told us it was right."

Brent, plane crash survivor, on how he and his sister-in-law overcame hunger as they desperately awaited rescue, 1979

Stranded in the snow-covered Idaho mountains, twenty-five-year-old Brent and his eighteen-year-old sister-in-law, Donna, found themselves with nothing to eat—except her dad, Don.

"He's dead but he wants us to live," Brent told Donna. "And he's given us his leather coat." Don handed the coat to Donna just before dying, unaware that she would soon take the body it had just been keeping warm. "We knew it was what Don would have wanted," Brent said. (Of course, what Don would have really wanted was for God to have intervened before the accident.)

The pilot also survived the crash but disappeared from the site in search of help. He was later found dead, but uneaten, a mile from the site.

Brent and Donna eventually reached safety after a five-day trek back to civilization.

The family had been on its way to a Boise kennel to pick up a puppy. The two survivors did not say whether they saved him one of Dad's bones.

HOLY ART THOU, HERMIT

"God told me that I must visit this church, as I have all the others, so that I could point out the errors and bring about the great reconciliation. He has chosen me His messenger to tell the peoples of the earth what is really true. I am the great comforter, I, sent by God: I am God's chosen messenger, and as such I am greater than the president of the United States, greater than the new-crowned King, and my message I will deliver."

Ernst, local hermit who lived outside of Sandfordtown, Kentucky, making one of many stops on his mission, 1911

Four years earlier, Ernst had wandered from New York to San Francisco, spreading the news that he was the latter-day Christ. He returned to his lonesome Kentucky cabin and took a long, much-needed break before emerging once again, reenergized, at the local church. There, he startled members as he walked down the aisle, clad in "picturesque home-made garments, with long, heavy flowing locks, and a bushy beard, half blonde, half gray."

Feeling mightier and more empowered than President Taft, he planned to journey through the South to deliver his message during the winter.

7TH-INNING SALVATION

"God spoke to me and said, 'You make a decision for me or you die.'"

Unidentified woman's response to her pastor's question: "You gave your life to Christ at a baseball game?" 1976

It was a Monday night at North Hollywood's largest Pentecostal church when the woman described her experience to the pastor and the exuberant audience. Enthusiastic hand-raising and shouts of "Hallelujah!" were a common sight at the services, as were tales of supernatural experiences, like the baseball game threat.

As the bleacher convert told her story, she downplayed the severity of the Lord's threat by saying, "Later, I felt He meant a spiritual death." Either way, you can add "grouchy" to the long list of terms to describe the Almighty. The woman abided and offered her life, but maybe all God really needed was a cold beer.

CLEANSE THY DRUG MONEY

"I prayed to God...because I wanted to know if I was supposed to [launder drug money]...God said that...He helped put this, this together. So I feel comfortable because of that."

Reverend David, on how he justified the laundering of $10 million in cocaine profits, 1995

Despite the Lord acting as the ringleader, undercover federal agents posing as members of a Columbian cocaine cartel still managed to fool the evangelical and his financial-advising co-conspirator. David tried explaining his actions to federal authorities as having been ordered by an even higher authority. He had been trying to pay off his church's debt, but when he asked parishioners to beef up their contributions, many left him. So he sought other means of finding the money and stumbled upon the undercover agents.

David's lawyer argued to the court that the reverend had been a victim of a government conspiracy. He claimed the agents fooled the reverend into thinking the money-laundering scheme would help him save his church. As such, he cried entrapment. Regardless, the unsympathetic jury found him guilty. Whether it was part of God's grand plan or not, an appellate court panel agreed with David and ultimately overturned his sentence of fourteen years in prison.

TOILET PAPER TABERNACLE

"God told me to [T.P. the police station]."

Unidentified man claiming to be Jesus Christ, on why he hurled toilet paper over trees outside a police station, 1993

Theologians may argue that God is as old as time; that He is eternal. Based on evidence from this case, He may actually be twelve.

God allegedly told this man—who called himself Jesus—to

vandalize the police station with toilet paper as revenge for what he called "false arrest." The man had been caught a day earlier urinating on and throwing eggs at a church but was later released from jail. However, his backpack had been confiscated. When he attempted to claim it the next day, he arrived after the property room had closed. Frustrated, he stole toilet paper from the station's men's room and set out to do the Lord's tomfoolery.

Police quickly spotted the hooligan and put a stop to the vandalism but not before the toilet paper decorated several trees.

"It was pretty good coverage," a police spokesperson said. "It was like Halloween."

Jesus was booked as John Doe and charged with second-degree criminal mischief.

HIGHER POWER HORSEPOWER

"I stand on what I know the Lord told me to do, whether anyone believes me or not...Never was I rude. I've never cussed anybody. I did raise my voice once calling on Jesus' name."

Marilyn, on her charges for trespassing at a Woodbridge, Virginia, car dealership and demanding a free vehicle, 2004

Despite multiple trespassing convictions in the previous year, Marilyn continued showing up at the dealership to demand a free car at God's request. When denied a vehicle, she refused to leave and was once again arrested. "That's where I was sent...I just go every time I'm ordered," she said. According to Marilyn's rationale, God's authority is higher than man's laws.

The judge in the case, although baffled, found the trespasser to be sane but seemingly confused. Marilyn was sentenced to thirty-six months in prison—all but one of which was suspended.

"I will not hesitate nor bat an eye to impose [the suspended thirty-five months jail time]," the judge told Marilyn. "I'm sure you can minister to a lot of people in jail, but if God's goal is for you to get a van, [you're not going to get a van in jail]."

FATHER'S FULL MONTY

"God told me to [be a male stripper]."

Robert, religious school teacher, on why he strips at night in the countryside of England, 1998

The English educator taught children Christian virtues of right and wrong during the day and transformed into Nick at night—strutting his God-given goods for the pleasure of screaming women.

While many opposed his lifestyle, the divorced father of three believes God defends it. "It even says in the Bible in the parable of the talents that you have a God-given duty to use what the Almighty has given you," Robert said. "Nowhere in the Bible does it say striptease is a sin. I'm just doing what I'm good at."

As far as the women he strips for are concerned, he's simply doing unto them what he would like done unto him.

HALLOWED HOOKER

"The Lord told me it's flat none of your business."

Jimmy Swaggart, addressing his congregation after being caught with his second prostitute, 1991

When a California highway patrolman pulled the famed TV evangelist over for driving on the wrong side of the road, he discovered Swaggart's distracted steering may have been because of the prostitute riding shotgun. Unfortunately for the preacher, the Lord didn't tell the officer that the situation was "flat none of his business."

Swaggart planned to step down from his pulpit the day after the incident but quickly changed his mind after a restless night of sleep. That evening he had tried reading the Bible to comfort himself, but the Good Book didn't do the trick: "I closed it and whimpered like a hurt little dog," he said. "'God, if you're there, if you're really there, tell me what to do.'" God told Swaggart to face his congregants but that he didn't have to explain himself. The next morning he did just that, and after telling his audience nothing, he invited them closer to the stage and asked them to pray for him. Hundreds of followers gathered on the stage, shouting prayers, chanting, and not once questioning his love of whores.

Just three years earlier, Swaggart had been caught in a motel with another hooker. He denied any intercourse during that encounter—she was only paid to "perform pornographic acts."

FALSE PROPHECY

"I heard the Lord saying, 'I have something else for you to do. I want you to run for president of the United States.' I assure you that I am going to be the next president of the United States."

Pat Robertson, religious broadcaster, during his presidential bid of 1988

Robertson has been chatting with God since the 1950s, when he received divine instructions to purchase a bankrupt UHF station. It eventually became the Christian Broadcasting Network and has spread to 180 countries, where it is heard in seventy-one languages.

Since that time Robertson's many conversations with the Lord have led to many not-so-accurate predictions over the years. Of course, in this case, Robertson may have simply misinterpreted the message. God said, "I want you to run." He didn't say, "I want you to win."

George H. W. Bush won the election in a landslide, while Robertson didn't even make it on the ticket. His campaign ended before the primaries were finished.

OMNIFICKLE

"Well, I guess God changed His mind. He twice told me I would die at 7 a.m. yesterday. I am greatly disappointed. I was ready to go."

James, after waiting twenty-four hours for death and waking in apparent good health, 1958

The sixty-nine-year-old Kentucky mountaineer had heard God beckon him to heaven while praying on the mountainside and had accepted this fate. Word spread quickly as James spoke of his upcoming death with great conviction. So convincing was the mountain man that the local funeral home had even made arrangements for his death.

His disappointment in waking up alive was shared by fifteen thousand members of the community—all of whom believed James would die and were moved by his faith. Five thousand people visited his home to witness the death—some coming from as far away as Tennessee, Ohio, Virginia, and Illinois.

Thankfully, not a single visitor attempted to prove God right after traveling all that way for nothing.

PETROL PRAYERS ANSWERED

"The Lord told me to put my hand on the gas gauge and talk in tongues. I started driving, and by the time I got half-way to where I was going, my gas tank was three-fourths full."

Danny, evangelist/faith healer, speaking at a revival meeting about one of God's recent miracles, 1982

Danny had found himself on the road with only a fifth of a tank of gasoline left in his car—not enough to complete his journey—and not a dime to spend on fuel. Had it not been for God's omnipresent pump, he would've never made it to his next revival.

The faith healer also shared other miracles with his crowd, including God's dentistry abilities. At an event that occurred just a few days prior, thirty people had fillings suddenly appear in their teeth.

"One lady had ten silver fillings appear," Danny said. "I believe the Lord fills old teeth...because if He just made new teeth nobody would believe it."

But will He also floss?

LAZARUS, ESQ.

"A vision from God told me that he would rise again."

Amandy, on why she worked all night to dig up the casket containing her divorce attorney, 1911

According to the Lord, if Amandy removed the earth covering her attorney's body and exposed it to air, he would rise from the dead. Once raised, he would surely sue the pants off whoever erroneously buried him.

But despite Amandy's efforts, she was unable to remove the lid after exhuming the casket from the grave. As dawn approached, she abandoned her task, but not before arousing people in the surrounding area. Amandy was found shortly after at the home of relatives and arrested on charges of desecrating a grave.

FAITH BLINDS

"While I was praying on my knees God told me to pick up the snake. I held him out in front of the congregation so they could see him. The snake turned slowly and bit me between the fingers...I picked him up again, and he bit me in the same place. He wouldn't turn loose this time."

Albert, hillbilly evangelist, on being poisoned and blinded by a snake during a radio broadcast to a national congregation, 1934

The thirty-nine-year-old evangelist gave his radio listeners an honest description of how it feels to be bitten by a rattlesnake to prove his faith in God as a healer. After the show, Albert went blind, lost movement in his jaw, and suffered nausea for the next day. He refused to go to a hospital, instead asking his congregation to pray.

Three days later, he recovered fully.

"Some persons have said that I would pick up another rattlesnake. I haven't said so...I wouldn't pick up another for all the money in the world unless God told me to," Albert said.

BABEL BABBLE

"When I was up in Heaven, God told me I could speak any language I wanted to, so one day after I came to this planet I went to a Chinese laundry, and I happened to remember what my Father told me, so I spoke to the Chinaman and he answered me. Then I tried the other languages and spoke 'em right off without even thinking."

William, patient at St. Elizabeth's Hospital, an institution for the insane, 1894

The Laundromat tale was just one of many wondrous adventures and experiences told to a visiting *Washington Post* reporter.

The self-proclaimed master of all languages claimed to have visited Venus, Mars, and Neptune, although he found no one there to speak to. William later took his family on a two-week trip to the moon: "We had a nice time. Nobody lives on the moon, and it's a pleasant place!"

His trip to the institution came, according to William, courtesy of the devil: "I was on a visit to God, my Father, and one day I went outside the heavenly gate, and Satan caught me and carried me off. He has claws and four horns and spits fire." But before being dropped off at St. Elizabeth's, Satan gave his prisoner a quick tour of hell. William didn't think it was too hellish, although he added, "But maybe I think that way because I didn't burn." He claimed there are nice people down there, including "some pretty women."

Before the reporter left, William extended an extraordinary invitation: "Say, miss, would you like to go with me next time, when I visit all the planets and Satan and my Father?"

She declined the offer, but in her article she wrote that this particular son of God was the most impressive patient she had visited.

SPANK THY LOVED ONES

"It came, 'Make paddles. Give them away.' God told me to make them. God's going to have to tell me to quit."

Joey, on why he makes spanking paddles to help parents discipline their children, 2007

Joey, a home remodeler, began making the Spanking Paddle after conversing with God while he showered. He tried to ignore the Lord's unusual demand: "I blew it off. The fourth time, it came real hard." So he obeyed. And since then, Joey's paddles, marked with the words "Never in anger," have been sent out to more than 1,300 parents with kids who need a good smack.

This holy entrepreneur doesn't believe in beating kids but believes they need appropriate discipline. His paddles include a self-written spanking manual, complete with a spanking schedule that helps parents know how many whacks to give and when. These guidelines, as directed by God, include one swat for being disrespectful and five swats for underage drinking. Joey also created appointment slips so parents and children can arrange a suitable spanking time for each offense.

Despite complaints from anti-spanking groups, Joey continues his duty: "I'm not trying to make money on it. I don't care about the money," he said. "I'm just doing what I'm supposed to do."

HAVE FAITH IN VIOLENCE

"There was this older lady worshipping right in front of the platform. And the Holy Spirit spoke to me. The gift of faith came on me. He said 'Kick her in the face. With your biker boot.' I went bam! And just as my boot made contact with her nose, she fell under the power of God."

Todd, evangelist, describing one of his many unorthodox methods of healing to his audience, 2008

Todd, an ex-con and former drug and alcohol abuser, changed his lifestyle and began his ministry at age eighteen. His faith healing has reportedly involved numerous kicks, punches, and other beatings. When he's not in the act of healing, he's demonstrating his methods on stage, engaging his audience with illustrative stomps and uppercuts into the air. He's rewarded with laughter and applause, as if it's nothing more than entertainment sponsored by God.

A one-week revival in Florida attracted as many as ten thousand attendees a night to witness his preaching. The night he described kicking the woman in her face with his biker boot, he also shared memories of punching out a

Chinese man's tooth, leg-dropping a pastor, and grabbing a crippled woman's legs and banging them "up and down on the platform like a baseball bat."

No "cures" have been medically documented.

LENNOX
FUBU

DON KING OF ALL KINGS

"So I said publicly that God told me I was going to knock him out in the third round. It didn't happen. And by the time the third round ended and I didn't knock him out, I began to lose energy."

Evander Holyfield, former heavyweight champion of the world, on his predicted victory over WBC champion Lennox Lewis, 1999

Holyfield shared God's words weeks before the championship fight scheduled at Madison Square Garden. The devout fighter's brazen prediction was in response to being called a hypocrite by Lewis for having several children out of wedlock (nine children with six women). "I thought that was none of his business, and he was ignorant about me. And I was mad," Holyfield said.

He was also upset over remarks that he was risking permanent brain damage by accepting the fight. But Holyfield had no fear, not with the ultimate cornerman watching his back: "I have confidence in the word of God. I'm not predicting, I'm telling you: I will knock him out in the third round."

The fight ended in a draw. Holyfield retained his title but later lost in a rematch.

LEND ME THY HAND

"He cut off his hand because God had told him to do so."

Police officer investigating a self-mutilation at a church, 1971

Obedient and fearless, James severed his left hand at the wrist with a hatchet, leaving only his right hand to carry out any further orders from God. Police found him behind a Baptist church; his hand was found in the garbage in a nearby alley. Say what you will about James, but he's no litterbug.

LEND ME THY ENTIRE ARM

"I purposefully put my left arm under the wheels of a street car in order to have it cut off. I was commanded by God to do this, and I did it of my own free will. I am not a drinking man."

Harry, describing in a sworn statement his reasons for severing his arm, 1913

The twenty-three-year-old claimed to be in full control of his sanity when sacrificing his arm to a trolley car in Buffalo, New York. "I knew and realized what I was doing," Harry said. He was treated at a hospital for shock and loss of blood. The trolley car was wiped clean and looked as good as new.

SURGICAL COMMANDMENT

"God told me that I had a religious medal in my stomach and that I should get it out with a knife before the world burst."

Edwin, explaining to detectives his reason for driving a fifteen-inch blade into his body, 1949

It all began when the forty-five-year-old woke up at one o'clock in the morning at his mother's house, where he lived, and opened a window to shout at God.

"God!" he yelled with all his might. Hearing no immediate answer, Edwin left the house and, according to reports, "addressed many words to the Deity" as he anxiously paced back and forth. His alarmed mother ran outdoors to help him, but Edwin had already gone back inside to carry out God's alleged response.

Edwin acted swiftly. By the time his mother returned to the house, she found him lying in a pool of blood on the floor—with not a single religious medal in sight.

Edwin was taken to a hospital in critical condition, and detectives held him on a breach of peace charge.

ALMIGHTY COMMANDER IN CHIEF

"I am driven with a mission from God. God would tell me, 'George, go and fight these terrorists in Afghanistan.' And I did. And then God would tell me, 'George, go and end the tyranny in Iraq.' And I did."

President George W. Bush, addressing a Palestinian delegation during an Israeli-Palestinian summit at an Egyptian resort shortly after invading Iraq, 2003

Bush happily listened to everything God told him. Unfortunately, he didn't pay much attention to the words of those who have preceded him and helped shape America—men like James Madison, who said in 1820, "Strongly guarded is the separation between religion and government in the Constitution of the United States."

UNGODLY MESS

"The Lord told me it was going to be (a) a disaster, and (b) messy."

Pat Robertson, on his warning to President Bush about invading Iraq, 2003

It would seem the Omniscient One would know that Pat Robertson didn't make the call on war. That honor went to God's other pal, George W. Bush, to whom He failed to mention either of the important war details He told Robertson.

Iraq statistics as of July 8, 2009:

* 4,325 U.S. soldiers killed
* 31,430 seriously wounded
* 139 journalists killed
* 9,126 Iraqi police and soldiers killed
* An estimated 100,000 Iraqi civilians killed
* $12 billion in spending per month in 2008
* $800 billion total spending

With Bush back in Texas, President Obama has taken on cleanup duty. In a June 2009 speech given before an Egyptian audience, Obama reached out to the Muslim world in an effort to restore America's image and explained policies regarding both Afghanistan and Iraq, including economic aid and infrastructure development.

Regarding Iraq specifically, he told his audience: "Although I believe that the Iraqi people are ultimately better off without the tyranny of Saddam Hussein, I also believe that events in Iraq have reminded America of the need to use diplomacy and build international consensus to resolve our problems whenever possible. Indeed, we can recall the words of Thomas Jefferson, who said, 'I hope that our wisdom will grow with our power, and teach us that the less we use our power the greater it will be.'"

It's sound advice for both nations and deities.

RUNNING ON A PRAYER

"There's only one explanation for it, and it's not a human one. It's the same power that helped a little boy with two fish and five loaves feed a crowd of five thousand people. That's the only way that our campaign can be doing what it's doing."

Mike Huckabee, former Arkansas governor, offering divine intervention as an explanation for his sudden success in the polls during his run for the Republican nomination for president, 2007

Toward the end of 2007, a surging Mike Huckabee spoke to a group of students at Jerry Falwell's Liberty University in Lynchburg, Virginia. When one of the attendees asked him what his rise in the polls could be attributed to, Huckabee gave his controversial explanation of Jesus's endorsement. However, he made no mention of his other recent celebrity endorser—Chuck Norris.

Despite alleged aid from the Son of God and campaigning from Norris, Huckabee soon saw his popularity fade and dropped out of the race. The power of prayer (and ass-kicking) simply couldn't compete with the presentation of ideas, foreign policy experience, charisma, and other qualities that generally win voters over.

THE PERILOUS HIGHWAY TO HEAVEN

"The Lord told me the spiritual overhead it's taking to keep you safe on these roads is very heavy, and I could keep you safer if you were tied down somewhere."

Former Colorado state senator Charles Duke, on why he quit his job as a trucker, 1999

Before God recommended Duke quit his trucking job, He advised him to leave politics. It had been a career marked by bizarre incidents, such as the time he accused Newt Gingrich of breaking into his townhouse and stealing his tax files, a pocketknife, and a part from his laser printer.

He later accused a congressman and his wife of conspiring to manipulate the stock market against him. "They are not doing it personally," Duke said. "They are asking the president to do it, and he's asking the Mafia. The Mafia controls the options rating and, as you know, the Mafia was created by the Rothchilds [sic] many centuries ago...[The congressman and his wife] have a lot to answer for, I'll put it that way, I'm leaving it in the Lord's hands."

The Lord's hands directed Duke out of his state senate

office and into a friend's home, where he occupied the space under the kitchen table and sat curled in a fetal position for three days. God helped him back on his feet, but He did not approve of Duke's move into the dangerous world of truck driving. After the Lord yanked him from his truck, Duke took a job at an undisclosed company.

X-RATED VISION

"And the Lord said, 'Ask her about her sex life.'"

Pat Robertson, on how God helped him simultaneously cure a woman's asthma and save her marriage, 2006

A woman came to Robertson complaining about her asthma, which doctors allegedly—and inexplicably—attributed to her praying with nuns. Robertson had the good sense to disagree with this diagnosis.

With God's intervention, he questioned the woman's sex life, which forced her to admit she had none because her husband was impotent. Prior to God's question, she had maintained her marriage was otherwise perfectly fine—but she had been blaming herself for her husband's impotence. Once Robertson assured her it wasn't her fault, they prayed to God to heal her asthma. According to Robertson, He did.

It is unknown whether the session also helped her husband overcome his problem, although exposing all the limpy details to a TV evangelist seems like an unlikely cure.

MONOCONSTITUENTISM

"He called me to run for the Minnesota state senate. I had no idea and no desire to be in politics. Absolutely none...God then called me to run for the United States Congress."

Congresswoman Michele Bachmann, describing how God had directed her career, 2006

"Who in their right mind would spend two years to run for a job that lasts two years?" Bachmann asked herself during her campaign. "You'd have to be absolutely a fool to do that. You are now looking at a fool for Christ."

The Lord first took interest in Bachmann's life when He introduced her husband to her in a vision. He later helped her through law school at Oral Roberts University, despite her initial lack of interest in law. Afterward, Bachmann's husband suggested a postdoctorate degree in tax law. She hated that too, but according to her, the Lord says, "Be submissive wives—you are to be submissive to your husbands."

Soon after, God's plan brought her into politics, where she's happily mixed in her faith with current issues, such as the environment. In speaking out against Nancy Pelosi,

Bachmann said, "[Pelosi] is committed to her global warming fanaticism to the point where she has said that she's just trying to save the planet. We all know that someone did that over two thousand years ago, they saved the planet—we didn't need Nancy Pelosi to do that."

In fairness, she told voters she was a fool before they elected her.

SODOM AND LOS ANGELES

"The Lord told me that between this year [1969] and 1974, California will face many disasters and by 1984 there will be no Los Angeles."

Reverend Gordon, leader of a California Pentecostal group who moved his entire congregation to Missouri, heeding God's warning, 1969

Gordon, along with one hundred congregants, made a new life in Independence, Missouri, safe from God's wrath. But they didn't follow the reverend's lead blindly—many of them also experienced visions with the same message. So urgent was the heavenly memo that one man gave away a seven-room home filled with furniture because he couldn't sell it fast enough.

As of this writing, Los Angeles is still thriving.

ELECTION INTERVENTION

"Just before President Clinton was elected in 1992, the Lord told me that He was placing a man in office who was not His choice. 'After Clinton, I will raise up a man like David,' the Lord said. 'A chosen man after My heart who will lead this nation in righteousness.'"

Hank, founder of One Voice Ministries, endorsing President Bush during the 2004 election

Hank continued to explain that God entered the political fray after the sinful Clinton administration to impose His will on America. "George W. Bush did not win the popular vote—he was not man's choice," Hank acknowledged. "The unusual circumstances surrounding the 2000 vote, including the endless recounts and the ruling by the U.S. Supreme Court, reminded us that God had intervened. I believe President Bush was God's choice."

So is God to blame for the second term too?

OUR FIRST LADY OF NO MERCY

"God has personally asked me to run for The Presidency Of The United States. He says no other Republican candidate can win...God has asked me to have [Laura Bush] be my running mate, my vice presidential candidate."

Gerald, psychic speaker and professional dishwasher, in his letter to Laura Bush, 2008

Gerald's relationship with God began at the age of seventeen after shooting a man in the groin. He had always been an ardent atheist, but while serving time for his actions, God introduced Himself, and the two have been in touch ever since.

When God, along with Jesus, compelled the North Dakota–based dishwasher to dive into the 2008 presidential race, Gerald did his darnedest to obey. He began his campaign by ordering pens with printed messages, such as "Save America." A website was launched to feature his political beliefs along with a series of letters to various politicians, journalists, psychic groups, and NFL teams. He even self-produced a host of radio and TV ads. And unlike traditional candidates who wait for their party's nomination, Gerald began the recruitment process of his running mate—sending Laura Bush more than seventy emails and copying the media. The First Lady never responded.

His campaign found itself in real trouble when Mrs. Bush visited a nearby school and failed to make a stop at Gerald's home to say hello and discuss strategy. "The thing that finally broke Jesus was that she was right here, she was just down the street, less than a block from us," Gerald said. "No invitation, no call, no nothing. All's Jesus wanted was a few minutes. That was when Jesus said, 'I'm done.' He went to God and tendered his resignation." Gerald alerted the media, officially ending the campaign on October 1, 2008. Laura Bush will have to explain her actions to Jesus later.

When not speaking with the Lord, the psychic and his wife channel dead celebrities. Both Jackson Pollock and John Lennon helped with his campaign—the former channeling a logo and the latter a song.

WHITE HOUSE OF THE LORD

"I believe it was Jesus' plan. Five minutes later, we decided to build the White House."

Fred, real estate developer and owner of the White House of Atlanta, 2009

It may have been Jesus's plan, but Fred's architect deserves credit (or blame) as well. After the developer's wife decided she wanted a house with columns, the architect offered the suggestion of replicating the White House—right in the middle of a residential Atlanta neighborhood.

Fred's White House is a third of the size of the president's but shares much of the opulence. Inside, the home boasts six bedrooms, numerous baths, a banquet room, a domed ceiling, and versions of the Oval Office and the Lincoln Bedroom, complete with a painted mural of Honest Abe and a copy of the Emancipation Proclamation. Outside, a cross stands tall before an enormous, meticulously designed topiary arrangement spelling out "God [hearts] you," and an adjacent fountain spouts water toward the heavens.

Fancy as it may be, Fred's neighbors aren't fond of it. "The White House is ridiculous and ostentatious to be among thirty-year-old homogeneous houses," one said. Another took issue with the claim that Jesus was involved: "I don't think God would want you to put millions of dollars into a White House for yourself when there might be some better uses for that money."

While the house is there to stay, Fred might not be. The housing market hit Atlanta hard in 2008 and Fred's bank tried to foreclose on the White House twice. He's managed to work around it, but has put the home up for sale at an asking price of $9.8 million. No wannabe presidents have made an offer, although Fred is not afraid: "If someone comes and gives me a good price, I will build a congressional building across the street." Or whatever else the Lord may recommend.

BLESSED ARE THE MINNESOTA VIKINGS

"Does God care? Evidently, He's cared sixteen times, because we won sixteen games, and not to say He didn't care the other two times, but maybe He cared enough to allow the other team to win the other two times."

Randall Cunningham, Minnesota Vikings quarterback, on the team's 1998 season

Cunningham may have felt God had been watching over him during this latter stage of his career, as just two years prior to his stint with the Vikings he had been out of football and laying tile in Las Vegas. He got the miraculous call to play again as a backup and took over in Week 2 after the starter suffered a leg injury.

The Vikings went 16–2 that season, losing in heartbreaking fashion to the Atlanta Falcons in the NFC Championship game. Though God appeared to prefer the Falcons, the Almighty fair-weather fan clearly cared about the eventual Super Bowl champion Denver Broncos even more.

TRAILER CRASH

"God told me to go down there, wake those people up and get them to church."

Jacob, on why he crashed his speeding car into a trailer park on a Sunday morning, 1963

Apparently, God said nothing about waking "those people" with a simple ringing of a bell or a trusty ram's horn. With the command left open to interpretation, Jacob sped his car at an estimated ninety miles per hour, plowing into the trailers and knocking them loose from their foundations. He succeeded in waking everyone inside, but failed miserably in getting them to church.

One woman suffered a back injury when the impact threw her out of bed, while others sustained bruises and were shaken up physically and mentally. "I was lifted off the chair and thrown to the floor," one of the residents said. "Then the furniture started flying around the trailer like feathers in a windstorm."

The county sheriff claimed it was a miracle that all eight occupants of the trailers were not seriously injured.

HUNGER SAVES?

"The Lord spoke to me on the street and told me to starve until Ernie joined the church. I will starve to death to save my husband."

Sadie, on Day 41 of her fast intended to influence her husband to join her church, 1921

A week later, Sadie ended her fast, claiming to have gone without food for forty-eight days. Yet a doctor examining her declared the fast could not have been longer than one week, stating her condition was virtually normal. Sadie was upset by the claim, saying it was an attempt to "cheat God of the glory of preserving my body and keeping me alive until the great victory is won."

During the fast, Ernie asked God if joining the church was right thing for him to do and if it would save his wife, but he was not given an answer. Left without divine guidance over the seven weeks, he repeatedly said, "I'll be damned if I give into her."

HUNGER DOTH NOT SAVE

"The Lord told me not to eat. I've got to repent for my sins. I can't eat again until I get an okay from God, Himself."

Joseph, thirty-four-year-old turret lathe operator, explaining his lengthy fast to local police, 1949

Unfortunately for Joseph, God never gave the "okay." After a 104-day self-imposed fast, his body gave up and death overtook him. The condition was apparently hereditary, as two years earlier, his father passed away after fasting for a relatively meager sixty days.

Joseph's only defiance of God's command came when a judge ordered him into a hospital to be fed intravenously. After a sanity hearing, a separate judge released him into his mother's care.

There, in her home, he continued to obey the Lord until he starved to death.

"I'm sorry this had to happen, but the boy thought he was doing right," his mother said, "and I agreed with him."

CURVEBALL FROM ABOVE

"God let him know that Brad was no longer supposed to play on the Buckskins team. He said God didn't want me on the team."

Brad, on the news he got from the Boise Buckskins baseball manager, after a 25–3 loss, 1978

The manager often prayed to God for advice on managing his team, usually receiving a response in a "crystal-clear voice, like you hear on the radio." This message came on neither AM or FM but as a gut feeling. "Well, He made it very clear to me and I called [the team owner], and it was confirmed to her in the Bible," he said.

The owner may have also been influenced by Brad's recent demand for more money, although she claimed all her answers regarding the team came from the Good Book. "I open up to a page in the Bible and look and the answer will be there," she said. "Sometimes if I don't get the answer, I try again—and open up to the same page."

HIGH WIRE TO HEAVEN

"As long as God lets me, I will walk the wire."

Karl, on his high-wire act, which ended with his deadly 120-foot plummet to the ground before hundreds of spectators, 1978

Karl, seventy-three, had performed on the wire for more than fifty years. During that span, he'd witnessed four members of his family die and his son suffer paralysis from the waist down while performing the same act. Deeply religious, he believed God walked with him on the wire. But on that fateful day, God was busy elsewhere—possibly managing a minor league baseball game in Boise, Idaho.

SPIRITUAL SHOPLIFTING

"To you I may appear a common thief, but this is not stealing. The Lord told me to take these goods."

Ruth, on why she stole red veils, red stockings, red ribbons, and red petticoats, 1913

When detectives arrested Ruth for stealing the merchandise from various downtown stores, she explained that she was merely acting under divine guidance. "The Master converses with me in words such as I am using with you now," she told the detective.

It wasn't the first time God had recommended a five-finger discount—Ruth had previously been picked up on shoplifting charges just three months earlier. After the first offense, the prosecution dropped the charges with her promise not to steal again. When reminded of her oath, she remarked that the merchandise had to be stolen as a test of her faithfulness in obeying God's word—which, of course, is a complete reversal of the eighth commandment.

BLIND ATTACK

"Ray Charles will see tonight. I did not choke him. I just placed my hands on him...God told me to do it."

Roger, on why he attacked the famous pianist and singer on stage at a Los Angeles benefit concert, 1977

Ray Charles was just one of many notable entertainers performing at the benefit concert for underprivileged youths and senior citizens. In the middle of his set, in front of a three-thousand-member audience, Roger calmly made his way on stage while reciting the Lord's prayers and then launched his attack. He managed to knock Charles's dark glasses to the ground before two brawny security guards yanked him away and foiled God's plan. "You will see, you will see!" Roger yelled as he was dragged offstage.

"Look at my hands. They are meant to heal, not hurt," he said. "This is a giant step for the poor of the world."

Rather than press charges and have Roger jailed, the concert's charitable host chose to give the man the help he clearly needed.

Charles was "shook up" but not badly injured. He remained blind.

THOU SHALT STIFF THY WAITRESS

"It was God's amusement to say, 'You little prig. Just walk out of there. Don't pay for the coffee. They'll survive, and this'll be good for you.'"

Norman Mailer, Pulitzer Prize–winning author, recounting why he once walked out of an all-night diner without paying, 2007

An atheist in his youth, Mailer spent his last fifty years contemplating the nature of God. During that time, he claimed God spoke to him on a few occasions, including the diner incident.

That night, Mailer had been bar hopping in hopes of picking up a woman. Unfortunately for him, he succeeded only in getting drunk and working up an appetite—both of which he treated at the diner. After eating a doughnut and finishing his coffee, the Lord encouraged the theft. "I was aghast," Mailer said, "because I'd been brought up properly. One thing you didn't do was steal." The voice persisted: "Go ahead and do it." So he did.

"My senses told me this was a divine voice, not a diabolical one," Mailer described. "It seemed to me that I was so locked into petty injunctions on how to behave, that on the one hand I wanted to be a wild man, yet I couldn't even steal a cup of coffee."

One can only wonder what sort of mischievous advice God would have given Mailer had he not wasted his early years with atheism.

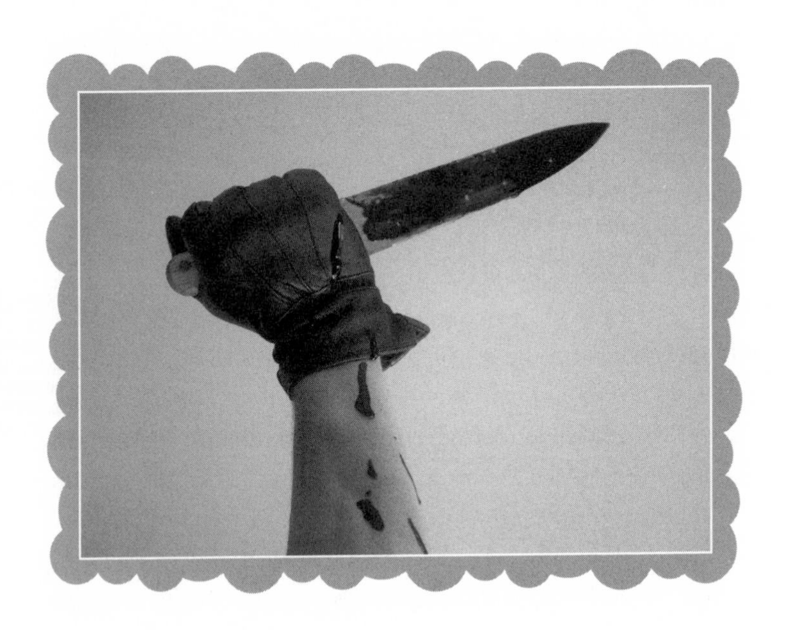

BEYOND CIRCUMCISION

"[Castration] was the right thing to do. God told me to do it all of a sudden. He has told me to do lots of things before."

Clyde, sawmill worker, on why he cut his brother's testicles off with a knife, 1935

Clyde performed the act at his brother Bob's home, in front of his sister-in-law and other witnesses. The sawmill worker struck him first with his fist and then pulled out a pocketknife to fulfill the Lord's commandment.

Clyde, a former professional fighter and former inmate of a state asylum, had no remorse for emasculating his brother, since he was only following God's request. There were no reports on what God asked Clyde to do with Bob's balls.

GOD'S REPUBLICAN

"The Angel of the Lord told me in January of 1992 that Hillary Rodham Clinton and I would meet and be running against each other and that she would lose."

Albert, a Republican from Michigan, writing on his presidential campaign website, 2007

Albert paid the $1,000 filing fee to appear on the New Hampshire primary ballot, thereby announcing his eligibility to become the next president of the United States.

Technically, the Lord's prediction was true. Albert was on the ballot against Hillary Clinton—and Clinton lost. God just didn't say anything about a victory for Albert.

SPREAD MY WORD AND THY CASH

"The Lord told her to [give $5,100 away to strangers]."

Julia, one of two elderly women who were abducted, robbed, and taken on a road trip to Washington to resurrect the perpetrator's brother from the dead, 1951

On that day, countless strangers gave thanks to God for their sudden spontaneous riches. The benefactors may have had other words for Him.

Both were forced to withdraw $5,100 in cash from the bank so the abductor, a young woman with "the most gorgeous auburn hair you ever saw," could distribute the money randomly "because the Lord ordered it."

"It was as if we had to do what she told us to…it was the will of God," Julia said.

No explanation was offered regarding the victims' roles in raising the younger woman's brother from his grave. Whether the cash giveaway was part of God's resurrection plan is also unknown. The culprit was apprehended and sent to an insane asylum.

SANTA LUCIFER

"I am doing God's work. I have been sent here by God to destroy Santa Claus, who has become an idol in your eyes. God has told me Santa Claus is the devil himself."

Billy, sidewalk preacher, who was arrested in San Antonio for destroying department store Christmas displays, 1961

The twenty-five-year-old Scrooge proved unsuccessful in harming Santa's reputation or preventing thousands of fat men from annually portraying the devilish idol in malls across America. In addition to Billy's failure, odds are he didn't get any presents that year.

NO DAILY BREAD

"He indicated to me my fast should be ended, so I asked how I should end it. He told me to drink squirrel soup. After I had taken the squirrel soup, I told Him it didn't taste good and asked if I could have some milk and bread. The Lord told me I couldn't have solid food yet as it would kill me."

Jackson, on his call from the Lord to end his fifty-two-day fast, 1937

The forty-five-year-old mountain trapper began his hunger strike at God's request, which came shortly after the Lord ordered him to sell his pigs and give the money to the poor. The sale facilitated the fast by eliminating all that tempting pork roaming outside the window.

However, Jackson's fast got off to a slow start: "The day after I started in, I took a little potato soup without grease. That learned me my lesson. I nearly died, it made me so sick. That was just the Lord punishing me for my disobedience."

When permission to sip squirrel soup ended his fast nearly two months later, Jackson expressed his great relief: "I'm mighty happy it's all over." But after the Lord told him to eat, He had nothing more to say. "The Lord's divine purpose has not been revealed to me yet, but it will be before long. Maybe he wants me to preach, if He does, I'm ready."

Jackson lost forty pounds during the ordeal. Perhaps the divine purpose was simply a diet.

THE GIFT OF SNACKING

"I was sitting in a restaurant, and the Lord revealed to me the idea of doubling up on the old recipe. It didn't make any sense, but I went ahead and tried it, knowing I had nothing to lose. When I poured it out, I had the most beautiful caramel popcorn I had ever seen! The Lord told me, 'This is the greatest gift I have ever given you. Now go!'"

Bill, founder of Heavenly Regal Blend popcorn, on how he struck gold with his caramel corn, 2008

God apparently had such a craving for this sticky snack that He convinced Bill to quit his job as a teacher to begin its creation. With the Lord at his side, Bill stopped filling the hungry minds of children and aimed straight for their stomachs instead.

He began by withdrawing his retirement money early and purchasing the various equipment needed for his new venture. Although risky, Bill claimed, "God said to me, 'Who do you trust more? The school district and state or Me?' I answered, 'Well, ok, Lord. If I trust you and you totally lead me and call the shots for my life, then let's see what you can do!'"

He found success and eventually earned the money to open a store, where he sells his homemade caramel almond popcorn based on the Lord's magic recipe. Beyond the store, his heavenly popcorn is available across the country at theme parks, tourist attractions, and one of God's favorite places, sports stadiums.

MOTOR CITY SAMSON

"He told me, although I had no money and was desperate, to build a $2,500 garage in my backyard and there, He said, I would invent something that would end all our material woes...a vehicle that will travel on land, water and in the air."

Robert, out-of-work welder, on what led him to lose his Detroit home and live in his car for three years, 1966

After losing his job, sixty-two-year-old Robert felt God's mighty finger tap him on his shoulder to offer His entrepreneurial career advice. Exciting as it sounded, the costly plan led to missed mortgage payments and the eventual loss of his home. He and his wife, Joanna, were forced to live as nomads in their two-door 1954 car, insulated with yellowing newspapers and packed with food tins.

Bearded and disheveled, Robert's woes grew larger when his car finally broke down three years later. Detroit police and welfare officials found him with literally a nickel to his name and just a few coins more to Joanna's. Yet, despite all the troubles, Robert held on to his faith in God. "My beard is my strength," he said. "Four years ago the Lord told me never to let scissors or a razor touch my hair. If only I could get back on my feet…earn enough to buy an acre of land and build a shack…I can obey His command and build my machine."

More than forty years later, Detroit is hoping God will tap someone else on the shoulder to help invent a better vehicle.

WANDERING AIMLESSLY IN THE DESERT

"God told me this year that the prayers are going to work."

Sister Martha, giving Arizona Cardinals fans much needed hope prior to the 2007 season at a local Kickoff Luncheon, 2007

At the time of the luncheon, the Arizona Cardinals had posted one winning season in the past twenty-two years. The club holds the NFL record for the longest championship drought and has successfully crushed fans' hearts for decades.

Would the presence of devout quarterback Kurt Warner—a former Super Bowl MVP—finally catch the Lord's attention? Would He stop casting Cardinals prayers aside like errant third-down passes and start paying attention to the woeful desert birds?

Nope.

The Arizona Cardinals missed the playoffs, finishing the season with an 8–8 record.

Sister Martha may not have given up hope, as God apparently answered the prayers a year later. In stunning fashion, the Cardinals made it to the Super Bowl after the 2008 season and nearly defeated the Pittsburgh Steelers. If only the Sister had been a Mother Superior—with a bit more pull Upstairs—her team may have ended its championship drought.

ROADSIDE BENEDICTION

"I was praying for the 18-wheelers and Volkswagens going by...And He told me, 'I want you to build a prayer stop.' I said, 'A what?' He said, 'These people you pray for don't go to church. I want to talk to them. If you'll build this, I will cause them to come in here.'"

George, Texas beer distributor, on why he built a small chapel on the side of the highway, 1983

George's fenced-in chapel, featuring a twenty-two-foot white cross, has hosted conversations between God and divorcees, alcoholic bums, millionaires, evangelists, monks, and motorcycle gangs.

It all began when the beer man spent an afternoon praying in the hills. "God said some pretty startling things to me," George said. "He told me I was just like everybody else, you know, just paying lip service to Him. I was crushed. I asked Him what He wanted me to do. He said sell everything you own and move to the country." George obeyed and bought a thirty-seven-acre farm with the earnings. The Lord even helped him get a good deal on the land: "God told me to offer him $10,000 less than the asking price." This new acreage gave him plenty of room to build God's prayer stop.

"Ever since it's happened, my life is full of joy, excitement and adventure," George said. Not to mention biker gangs and drunken bums.

LUMBERJESUS

"I was in my work truck...when God told me to [use toothpicks to build a life-sized Jesus]. I said, 'Gee, I can't do that. You're asking me to undertake a task that will take ten years.'"

Bob, on why he built a statue of the crucified Christ in his garage, 1991

Bob, who had no formal art training and nerve damage in his left hand from a recent jackhammer incident, cast his doubts aside and armed himself with tweezers, Super Glue, and sixty-five thousand toothpicks of the round, flat, square, and sandwich variety to create his wooden masterpiece. Not to mention five years of his life (only half his original estimate). Being divorced and having lost his job toward the end of the project helped him find time.

Still, building a Jesus out of toothpicks was no easy task. Bob managed to conquer numerous creative challenges along the way but was nearly stumped at the very end. "For five years, I never knew how to do the hair," he said. "About two weeks ago, I was sitting on the stool looking at it, and I was frustrated and I said, 'Lord, I've worked on this thing five years, how am I going to do the hair?' I had a thin, flat toothpick, and a thought came to me to bend it and lay it on the head." God wasn't about to let hair screw things up.

The sculpture was suspended by wire in his garage and illuminated with a spotlight. Bob called it "The Gift," a name he claimed God suggested. "I think I know what [God's] doing," he said. "He wants to inspire people." Anyone who's ever doubted their own toothpick artistry will agree.

THE PARTING OF THE PUDDLES

"The street became flooded. I got down on my knees and said to the Lord: 'You know that the soles of my shoes are thin, and if I go out I will get my feet wet.' The Lord said: 'Go!' I left my house during the storm and walked several blocks to this sanctuary. When I arrived the soles of my shoes were as dry as when I left home."

Elderly woman describing how she was able to make it to a convocation at her church despite stormy weather, 1903

The woman claimed to fellow churchgoers that she did not wear rubbers over her shoes, and her clothes remained dry through her journey. She did not, however, mention whether she carried an umbrella.

SEEKERS OF THE LOST ARK

"I was ordered by God to kneel down and pray. Since then, I had three heart attacks and underwent cardiac surgery twice. You see, I am not permitted to die but was given new opportunities to find the ark."

James, ex-astronaut, on what God told him in 1971 when he walked on the moon, 1986

James explained his divine mission to find Noah's ark at a press conference in the town of Erzurum, in eastern Turkey. A religious fundamentalist, James was making his fifth attempt to find any remains of the ark on Mt. Ararat, where the Bible claims it landed when the flood subsided. His team of seven included an eighty-one-year-old explorer who climbed the 17,011-foot volcanic mountain twenty-one times.

According to scientists, James's quest may be futile. Many claim there is no geological evidence supporting a flood burying the earth to the level necessary for the ark to end up atop Mt. Ararat.

Perhaps this is why God—who helped James find his way to the moon and ordered Noah's voyage—can't find the ark there either.

LESBIAN SEX SHALL BE FORBIDDEN IN THE LIBRARY

"God was speaking to my heart that day and helped me find the words that proved successful in removing this book from the shelf."

Earl, concerned father, on removing *The Whole Lesbian Sex Book* from his local library, 2007

Earl's fourteen- and sixteen-year-old sons took it upon themselves to learn about the alternative birds and bees at their local library. But when the lesbian literature was found at home, the rest of the family went into a state of shock.

Armed with God's help, Earl filed the necessary form to have the book banned, thereby censoring the library and ensuring no one in the community could study lesbianism. He also threatened to sue the city for $20,000 to pay for the mental damage to his boys. The story went public, and the library received an outpouring of support from all across the country.

Ultimately, Earl never followed through with the lawsuit, and after a thorough review, the library staff determined the book deserved to remain on the shelf.

With the book-banning efforts behind him, Earl can focus on making sure his pubescent boys don't discover the wonders of the Internet.

EXALTED PICKUP

"My husband and I have been praying for a truck and I believe this is what God wants us to do."

Norma, runner-up in the 1994 Hands on a Hard Body contest held in Longview, Texas, on how she had planned to get her new pickup truck

Norma, featured in the 1998 documentary *Hands on a Hard Body,* nearly won a new truck simply by standing next to it and keeping one hand on it at all times. Twenty-two other contestants also placed a hand on the 1995 Nissan pickup hoping to be the last one standing and taking the hard body home as a prize.

The day Norma learned she won an entry into the competition, she sold her old vehicle, fully believing the Lord had heard her prayers. "We have a prayer chain at the church and even people that aren't on there are praying for me," she said. A friend who attended the event to cheer her on added, "In Longview, about fifty families are praying. And her family in San Antonio. Conservatively, there could be about two hundred people praying. Counting children and husbands."

Norma spent the majority of the contest wearing headphones blasting gospel music in her ears. But in the end, after more than seventy hours and with only one other competitor left standing, Norma clapped her hands to the music.

The other guy won the truck.

1040
Label
(See
instructions
on page 12.)
Use the IRS

THE LORD'S LOOPHOLE

"The Lord told me not to pay income taxes."

Charles, telling the jury at his trial why he was excused from every American's favorite duty, 1979

Charles was sentenced to one year in jail and later admitted to the judge that he was wrong. The Lord offered no such apology.

15
15
100
5
90
90
25

THE BIG WHEEL IN THE SKY

"The Lord told me to bid $19,500. The audience roared because they thought I underbid. The actual price of my showcase was $20,000, and I won."

Roger, military information manager, on how he won *The Price is Right*'s Showcase Showdown, 2004

Roger's road to game-show glory began with his third bid in Contestants' Row, where he won a fabulous new dishwasher. He played poorly in the game that followed but managed to hit $1 when he took his spin on the Big Wheel, earning him one of the coveted Showcase Showdown slots. When God came on down to Roger's aid, he won two motorcycles, a dinette set, platinum china, and a home-alarm system.

"I was praying to God to please show me a miracle. It was a blessing for me to win the showcase," Roger said.

Of course, the true miracle was hearing God's voice over the always-boisterous audience.

THE END WAS NEAR

"The world ends next year. There is no time to waste. Some of our leaders talk directly to God. Any minute from now when the end comes, every believer who will be at an as yet undisclosed spot will be saved."

Emmanuel, nineteen-year-old member of the Movement for the Restoration of the Ten Commandments of God cult in Uganda, which ended with the murders of more than eight hundred members, 1999

Leaders of the movement, founded in the late 1980s by a former Catholic priest and a former prostitute who had a vision of the Virgin Mary, told members the world would end on December 31, 1999.

Three months after the world didn't self-destruct, more than three hundred members were killed in a fire set in a church. Police believed the leaders lured followers in before starting the blaze. Weeks later, another fifty-three bodies were found beneath a recently poured concrete floor in the home of one of the leaders. Hundreds of others were found nearby, either poisoned, stabbed, or strangled.

One theory for the mass murder suggests that members had

been asked to sell everything before the end of the world and give the sales income to the church. When the sun rose on January 1, 2000, and on the days that followed, doomsday-wishers may have demanded a refund.

THE UGANDAN MOSES

"God sent me as his prophet to tell his people to follow the new Eighteen Commandments which have replaced the old Ten Commandments for the New Jerusalem. The Creator told me five things will happen as a sign of the end of the world before the last judgment is passed on to people."

Francis, cult leader of the New Jerusalem Church in Uganda, 2007

Just eight years after the Movement for the Restoration of the Ten Commandments of God massacre, the Ugandan police showed little tolerance toward any doomsday groups. When locals tipped off the authorities to the latest cultish shenanigans, Francis was quickly arrested.

The cult leader claimed God informed him there would be five punishments leading up to the end of the world: epidemics (AIDS), famine, earthquakes, heavy rains with giant hailstones, and angels burning sinners around the world. At the time, Uganda was suffering from a series of massive floods.

Perhaps this doom-and-gloom worldview is what led Francis to seek a glimmer of light, claiming the new eighteenth commandment stated: "Sex is a holy gift and should be shared and enjoyed by all."

THE KING DETHRONES THE EMPEROR

"God wanted me to rule thirty years as an Emperor. Then He discarded me and allowed me to be dethroned, perhaps to try whether my faith would be shaken. It is not."

Kaiser Wilhelm II, speaking about his abdication of the German throne in 1918, following Germany's loss in World War I, and during the German Revolution, 1927

A religious man, Kaiser Wilhelm II ruled with God as his personal advisor. He believed that Germany lost World War I because "we did not obey God in all things; because we hesitated to bear the worst; because we refused in the end to face all risks in preserving faith!...We should have fought to the very last carrot, the very last man, the very last round of ammunition."

So strong was the kaiser's faith, he believed that had Germany fought harder, it could've prevailed—even if its army had been outnumbered twenty to one: "We should have trusted in God, not in human logic."

For World War II, Germany put its trust in neither.

THOU SHALT HIT OVER AND OVER AND OVER AGAIN

"God didn't say to mutilate her. He just said to hit her until she was dead."

Harvey Louis Carignan, known as the Want-Ad Killer, explaining to the court why he eventually stopped hitting his victim when he erroneously thought she was dead, 1975

Known as the Want-Ad Killer (having lured victims from the want ads), Harvey Louis Carignan of Fargo, North Dakota, murdered at least five people, possibly up to eighteen, in at least four different states from 1949 until his arrest in 1974. After kidnapping, beating, sexually assaulting, sodomizing, raping and/or choking his victims, he used a claw hammer to kill them.

Carignan described himself as "an instrument of God, one who was acting under His personal instructions." Imagine if he'd been working under the devil's instead.

AND YE SHALL FEAST ON HER FLESH

"God told me to [cook my girlfriend]."

Christopher, aka the Texas Cannibal, on why he killed his twenty-one-year-old girlfriend, mutilated her body, and cooked parts of her flesh, 2008

After the murder, Christopher invited his mother and her husband to come see what he had done. Horrified, they quickly fled the scene and called 911. Christopher called the police as well, and informed the dispatcher of his dinner plans.

Investigators found the victim's body with chunks of flesh missing, one of her ears boiling in water, and a portion of flesh with a fork in it sitting on the kitchen table.

Yet when God spoke to another killer, Harvey Louis Carignan, He specifically said not to mutilate, opting instead for repeated hitting.

CRUCIFIXATION

"At no point was it ever conveyed that I would definitely be crucified...Having experienced the humility of bearing my own cross through the streets, I felt my God wanted me only to pray at the foot of my cross."

Dominik, British journalist, on why he backed out of his own planned crucifixion in the Philippines, 2006

Dominik had planned to join an elite group of extreme Roman Catholics who celebrate Easter by reenacting the Crucifixion. Britain's Channel Five followed with cameras to produce a documentary of the event. But after watching nine Filipinos volunteer to be nailed to crosses with metal spikes and then get whipped, Dominik got the word from God that he shouldn't do it. The thousands of locals and tourists who had gathered to watch began to boo. Dominik wept.

Had he followed through with his mission, he would've been the second Westerner to do so. The first, a London oil painter, went through the crucifixion to experience the pain for artistic reasons. "I'm glad he bottled it. I mean, going over there with a Channel Five crew is not right.... This is very special to these people. It is something they do to get closer to God, not something that should be cheapened," the artist said. "I tell you, it really hurts having nails driven through your hands."

CONTEMPT FOR COURT

"God wants me to destroy the judge. That judge is evil. He wants me to get rid of her."

Robert, while awaiting sentencing for a tax evasion conviction, 2008

After his comments were recorded on a prison phone, Robert, a former CEO of a computer parts company, was indicted on charges of obstruction and conspiracy to impede justice.

If he couldn't destroy the judge as God suggested, he at least hoped to cause a ruckus in her courtroom by ordering dozens of people to disrupt his trial if the charges weren't dismissed. They didn't show up.

Robert believed only Jesus has jurisdiction over people, but he soon discovered that a jury in a federal court had even more power than the Son of God—at least in this case. He was found guilty of obstruction of justice for his threats and was sentenced to four years in prison. Robert's tax evasion conviction previously earned him eleven years, giving him plenty of time to question God's desires and Jesus's authority.

DEMONS WITHIN AND AROUND

"The Lord told me to bind him hand and foot and cast him into outer darkness. I tied his hands and feet but he chewed up the strings and I tied him again. He died the next morning."

Paul, on how his twenty-six-year-old crippled brother, Grant, died after being starved and abused in order to "drive out the devils that possessed him," 1932

Big brother Paul kept a diary about the efforts he and his mother put forth to drive the devil out of the poor cripple, like starving him. God had assured them that would take care of the demonic issue. That and tying him up.

According to the diary, Grant died on April 4 but was predicted to rise from his grave on June 24. However, like every date before and after the 24th, there were no reported sightings of the living dead.

BEHOLD AND BEHEAD

"She was fighting. I cut her head off and I walked away. God spoke to me and said, 'When you slay, slay. Cut off the left leg, the right leg.'"

Rosario, on the murder of his ex-girlfriend and mother of his then six-year-old son, 2004

God's how-to instructions came only after His initial command for Rosario to kill both his ex and his eighty-eight-year-old grandmother. The message came to this pious soldier while he was listening to religious tapes on a drive from Newark to Asbury Park.

"The communication told me to go to the house and kill the two people," Rosario testified. "I'm like, 'Dude, I'm not going to kill these people. That's a negative. No shot.'" But God can be very persuasive. Rosario, armed with a meat cleaver and a kitchen knife, carried out his orders once he reached the home where both women lived.

Upon arrest, the murderer explained to detectives that he was taking care of God's unfinished business dating back more than five hundred years, when the Lord ordered the deaths of the descendants of a Middle Eastern king. He claimed his grandmother was one of the descendants. Like his ex-girlfriend, she was beheaded. "She was trying to fight me, but she's very frail," he said.

Rosario was so caught up in decapitation and the severing of limbs, it apparently never occurred to him that he, like his grandmother, was also a descendant of the king in question. After all that, God's mission remained unfinished.

HOLY WAR OF THE WORLDS

"The Lord specifically led me into what I have termed the Alien Agenda and has revealed much information to me about the coming UFO and Alien invasion to America and our Earth."

Sherry Shriner, author of *Bible Codes Revealed*, on what God told her through codes, 2002

Shriner is God's ambassador to UFO junkies. She preaches her message through books, twelve websites, and an

Internet radio show, which is broadcast to more than one hundred countries.

According to Shriner and her divine source, an alien cover-up has been ongoing since the Eisenhower administration, when the president secretly signed a formal treaty with extraterrestrials. But apparently, that quiet collaboration with the little green men is about to get loud and nasty. The Lord told her so. He's also mentioned some other really awful upcoming events. In addition to being invaded by aliens—which God either didn't create or simply doesn't like as much as us—Shriner has also warned of the Luciferian New World Order and the Antichrist coming to power.

Thanks to her many efforts, the world will be ready when the aliens, Luciferians, and Antichrist come.

GRAND PRIX-CHER

"I am not planning any more stunts. God told me this was my defining moment."

Neil, defrocked priest, after his sudden dance on the fastest stretch of the British Formula 1 Grand Prix circuit, 2003

Drivers were forced to swerve out of the way at speeds of up to 200 miles per hour to avoid running over Neil (and ruining their chances of winning the race). Dressed as a leprechaun with a sandwich board urging onlookers to "Read the Bible, the Bible is always right," the former priest danced a jig amidst the racecars without an ounce of fear. This "defining moment" was seen by millions of television viewers watching in both horror and amusement.

"I did not think I could die. I had the Bible in my top pocket and I felt it and the hand of God were protecting me, the drivers and the public," Neil said.

He served a two-month jail sentence for aggravated trespass.

One year later, Neil traveled to the Olympic Games in Athens and attacked the lead marathon runner, dragging him to the ground just three miles from the finish line. He apologized in court and said he hoped to be forgiven on Judgment Day.

OMG, WTF GOD?

"God's text messages told me to kill."

> Sara, nanny and murderer, on why she shot her employer's wife and attempted to kill a neighbor, Sweden, 2004

Helge, a local reverend who was tired of his depressed wife, sought comfort from Sara, his children's twenty-seven-year-old nanny. That comfort came in the form of sex every night—with

Helge convincing her it was God's will. "Every sex act was a victory for God," Sara testified.

Soon after the affair began, the naughty nanny received a series of anonymous SMS messages urging her to kill Helge's wife, which she believed came from God. Of course, God is way too old for texting. Her lover had been sending the messages, and Sara received them loud and clear, promptly attempting murder with a hammer blow to his wife's head. The wife survived, and now it was the reverend's turn to be depressed. He sent Sara nearly two thousand text messages pushing her to finish the job. Rather than continue to rack up text charges, Sara returned with a gun and finished what she started.

With his wife out of the picture, the reverend wanted to pursue a second affair he'd been having with his neighbor, Anette. However, she had a husband standing between them, meaning Helge had more dirty work for his nanny to do. He manipulated Sara to take her gun and remaining bullets and kill Anette's husband too. But like Helge's wife, he survived the attack. Afterward, the reverend informed Sara that she was "a reprobate minion of the Devil."

If only Sara had hit "reply" to God's messages, perhaps she could've confirmed whether they were received in heaven or a nearby hell.

BIBLE MOBILE

"The Lord laid it in my mind to paint pictures from the Bible and words from Bible on my car so the children could understand the pictures maybe and get grown-ups' attention and they'll read it. Sometimes that's the only Bible people read during the day or sometimes in their life is when they stop long enough on the street to look at it."

H. L., artist, on why he adorned his pickup truck with all things Jesus, 1992

H. L.'s biblical pickup was featured in the 1992 art car documentary, *Wild Wheels*, where he explained his artistic mission.

A large image of Jesus surrounded by flowers adorns the hood, while biblical passages and images are emblazoned around and inside the entire vehicle, even on the steering wheel. The popular phrase "Jesus Saves" is implied with a life preserver attached above the rear wheel sporting the words "Jesus Ahoy."

"I used the talent He gave me because I love to paint and draw and I love to glorify the Lord." H. L. said. "It's better that I glorify the Lord than to glorify myself. Because there ain't nothing about me worth glorifying. Without Him I ain't nothing. The word Christian is C-H-R-I-S-T-I-A-N. The I-A-N is 'I ain't nothing' without Christ.'"

H. L. also enjoyed painting James Dean.

CHURCHYARD SHELTER

"God wants me [to live outside the church in a cardboard home]...I'm living God's will."

Jim, on why he and his dog spent thirteen months squatting in the front yard of their Akron, Ohio, church, 1996

Church members initially welcomed Jim's makeshift home, but as time passed, they began to reconsider their generosity. The cardboard lodging was secured with duct tape and, like similarly constructed dwellings, was not equipped with any means to shower. Bearded and outfitted in patched clothing, Jim slept in a soiled sleeping bag and refused an offer of a clean replacement claiming it wasn't God's will to be concerned with sanitation. Food was only accepted if it was given in response to God.

When six-inch rats joined Jim and found their way inside the church, disturbed congregants finally asked God for guidance on how to handle the holy squatter. But whose side would the Lord take?

"This is a lose-lose situation," said the church's reverend. "If God called Jim to live in our front yard, who are we to say God didn't?" His congregants finally overruled God's alleged word and voted to evict Jim from the church grounds.

OMNIPRESENT WITNESS

"God told me Jimmy Hoffa paid $1.5 million to have John F. Kennedy killed."

Glenn, telephone-pole creosote salesman, informing the FBI of his scoop from the Almighty, 1977

FBI agents responded to Glenn's information, which promised to solve one of America's great mysteries—and which came from the ultimate witness.

Upon traveling to Philadelphia to get all the vital Hoffa details, investigators described Glenn's message from God: "He told of his being in his room at the Ben Franklin Hotel, Philadelphia, PA...and while in the bathroom a light came through the transom and a voice spoke...He told of being so frightened he fell to the floor and held onto the bathroom fixtures."

Glenn received no future messages on where to find Hoffa's body.

REALITY SHOW INTERVENTION

"If everything pans out as God's told me it's going to, I will win POV tomorrow, and Jameka and me will be in the final two; I just know it."

Amber, *Big Brother 8* contestant, on God's involvement in the game, 2007

According to Amber, God was among *Big Brother*'s millions of fans and used His omnipotence and influence to help determine the outcome of the show. However, God apparently tuned out, stepped away for a snack, or got hooked on one of the many other reality shows because Amber was evicted from the house and failed to make it into the final two. Or was God just playing the game like the other contestants? Lying and backstabbing is what the show's really all about.

Jameka was also evicted before reaching the final two.

30-FOOT LEAP OF FAITH

"God told me to climb the building."

Jack, shouting his reason for scaling New York City's landmark Ansonia Hotel, half-naked, before falling thirty feet onto a police air bag, 1997

The Lord chose a cold January day for the overweight Jack to strip down to his underpants and tank top before climbing the hotel's stone façade. A crowd quickly gathered, including a group of women praying in a circle for him. But while they prayed, Jack waved his arms wildly and continued shouting about God. The Lord was forced to choose sides: Should He continue to make the semi-nude, fat guy climb or listen to the ladies and bring him down to safety?

Police intervened and kept Jack talking while an air bag was brought to the premises. Eventually, he lost his grip and plunged safely to the center of the cushion. Score one for the prayer circle.

JUDAS GOES TO COURT

"God told me to testify against O. J."

Walter, former defendant in the O. J. Simpson kidnapping and armed robbery case, on why he decided to take the stand in court, 2008

Armed with a .22-caliber pistol, Walter stood at Simpson's side during the former football star's chaotic attempt to reclaim allegedly stolen memorabilia from a Las Vegas hotel room in 2007.

The accomplice accepted a plea deal in the case, deciding to testify against Simpson. "I prayed on the matter and I had a revelation that I did something wrong, and the Bible told me I should go tell the truth," Walter told Simpson's lawyer. When asked if God had spoken to him, he replied, "Yes."

Of course, the prosecution's promise of reduced charges also aided his decision.

Simpson was sentenced to a maximum of thirty-three years.

KING SOLOMON OF SUSSEX

"God told me to live like a king."

Philip, secondhand furniture salesman, on why he's taken seven wives, Brighton, Sussex, 2006

Philip, who was once a rabbi in the Messianic Jewish Church (they follow Jewish teachings and also believe in Jesus), claimed a series of visions told him to take multiple brides, like King David and King Solomon. With the Lord's help, he gathered a stable of women, ranging from twenty-seven to sixty-two years old. Although not legally married to any of the ladies, he does have sex with each, choosing whichever partner he craves on a nightly basis. Five children have joined the full house, born to three different wives. Philip's four used-furniture shops and a horse training business help support the loving brood.

The pious polygamist hopes his harem will help break down equal rights and pave the way to a world where all women bow to their men. "It's about men having a status of headship over women," he explained. "Today, most women want to rule the roost. I will not live that way."

His wives enjoy the arrangement but admit certain

difficulties. "Being one of seven wives draws out all your insecurity, jealousy and stupidity," said forty-seven-year-old Judith.

When not reading Jewish scriptures and pleasuring their master, the women scrape up horse droppings while Philip supervises on horseback. No writings indicate that this was also customary with the ancient Hebrew kings.

UNDRESSED TO KILL

"God wanted me to drive naked."

Taliyah, explaining to police why she was in the buff after she struck another vehicle, killing its driver, 2006

In addition to driving clothing-impaired, Taliyah was also under the influence of Ecstasy and marijuana. God guided His nude driver in her Nissan Maxima on the wrong side of the road with her headlights off at 100 miles per hour.

Taliyah was found guilty of second-degree murder, reckless endangerment in the first degree, and driving while intoxicated.

Although her car was totaled, it seemed God really was on her side—Taliyah walked away from the accident with only a cut on her ankle.

STREET SOVEREIGN

"The Lord told me I no longer needed car insurance."

Peter, preacher, explaining his numerous motoring charges to a court, South Wales, 2001

Peter faced charges of driving his Ford Sierra without insurance and for owning an unlicensed plate marked "DEUT 818," referencing the Old Testament book of Deuteronomy. The verse claims that God is the only source of power—way beyond the petty rules of the road.

After the hearing, Peter said, "I told the police I traveled with God as my passenger. I have been licensed from Heaven, and I will be giving the word of the Lord in court. They will have to accept God is on my side."

The court did not accept Jehovah as a witness. Peter was found guilty on all charges and fined.

SUPREME PUPPET MASTER

"The word He impressed upon me was to get out there on street corners wherever people may be and let that dummy warn His people that our Lord and Savior is coming soon."

Poor Penny, ventriloquist, on why he left his entertainment career in Los Angeles, 2007

Armed with a megaphone, a sandwich board covered in prophetic scriptures from the Book of the Revelation, and a dummy named "Sweet Pea Johnson," Penny has preached the coming of the Rapture on street corners of small towns across America for more than thirty years. He's taken his dummy and his message to all forty-eight continental states—twice.

Penny likens himself to Noah, who was also dismissed as crazy and laughed at when warning of God's plans.

WANDERING TO AND FRO

"God told me that I should dress funny and walk across the United States."

Nick, on why he walks from town to town, visiting churches dressed as biblical characters, 2008

Nick preaches that people must discover what they're best at and put it to work for God. In his case, it's walking and talking.

The funny dresser made his first cross-country trek in 2001, walking from St. Augustine, Florida, to Garden Grove, California. According to his wife, Lucy, the trip took thirteen months and just as many pairs of shoes. He made a second journey in 2005, which lasted fourteen months and required eighteen pairs of shoes. "We had tried to use cheaper tennis shoes, but the road ate them up," Lucy explained. While her husband walked in full costume, she drove alongside in an RV—a mobile closet for Nick's entire biblical wardrobe, which surely included a coat of many colors for those long, cold winter months.

MODERN-DAY METHUSELAH

"God told me I didn't do nothin' wrong. Demons talk to me. God told me this 30,000 years ago. Who are you people who keep saying I'm a bad person?"

Ivan, aka "The Urinator," convicted armed robber, pleading his innocence in court, 2008

After forty-nine total arrests and an earlier incident in court in which he wet his pants and claimed to be twenty thousand years old, a judge finally took Ivan off the streets once and for all.

The ancient Urinator was sentenced to forty-three years in prison for holding up a video game store—and threatening all those inside—just before Christmas 2003. Claiming all he wanted "was games for his kid," Ivan stole 137 of them, along with more than $1,000 in cash.

Ivan proceeded to tell the judge, "God told me to write you a letter. You're the master demon, the demon in black."

Despite The Urinator's unusual actions and statements in court, three mental professionals determined he did not qualify for an insanity plea.

CROSS WALK

"The Lord put it on my heart to carry a cross across the United States, from Florida to California."

Lance, traveling evangelist, on his cross-country ministry mission, 1996

Although he dressed as Jesus, complete with a long, brown beard, and carried a ten-foot cross, Lance made no claim to be the Son of God. He was just a guy wandering America spreading his message through a form of visual evangelism. Wandering with him were his wife and four children, traveling at his side in a motor home.

Along the way, Lance spoke with those who stopped to ask questions, offered prayers for those in need, and occasionally defended his actions against those who criticized him. He also witnessed the birth of his fifth child, who was born in the motor home and weighed on the checkout scale at a nearby K-Mart.

Traveling across America was nothing new to Lance and his wife. They had already been roaming the land since 1988 in a 1971 Ford bus, given to them for free by a pastor and marked with the words "Chapel on Wheels." It was exactly what the evangelizing nomad had been looking for. After finding religion, Lance felt his faith in the Lord should provide security, rather than more common means, like a job.

"What if the Lord brought us a bus and we just took it on the streets and witnessed to people, and lived for the Lord?" Lance asked his wife. She agreed, on the condition that God provided a bus.

Sure enough, God delivered the Chapel on Wheels. Like any new abode, the first order of business was renovations, which included a wood-burning stove, a bathroom, a kitchen sink, an insulated floor, and a mailbox.

With his bus-driving days over and his 2,600-mile cross-country cross-carrying mission complete, Lance took it upon himself to keep walking. Toward the end of 2001, he embarked on a prayer walk up the Mississippi River, training those he encountered in his unique form of evangelism and unquestionable faith.

HE MADE THE MAID DO IT

"The Lord told me to kill them all, and I'm glad I got one of them...Why should I be sorry when the Lord told me do it?"

Mary, maid, on killing her employer and attempting to kill the rest of his family, 1924

The maid appeared to snap early one morning as the family she worked for slept. At 2:30 a.m., she walked down to the cellar, grabbed an axe, and tiptoed up to her employer's room. Standing over his bed, she brought the axe down across his throat, killing him nearly instantly. She struck him four more times for good measure.

A brief shout at the first hit woke his wife and daughter, who slept in an adjacent room. The wife, ill, remained in her bed while his daughter entered the room to investigate. Still crazed with the Lord's instructions, Mary swung at the girl, grazing her cheek as she fled for help. The helpless wife was not so lucky. Mary struck her throat, chest, and nearly severed her foot.

Police quickly came and subdued the murderer after a lengthy struggle. "God told me to kill them and I'm not going to run away," Mary told them.

UNREAL ESTATE

"The Lord told me someone would give us a building, FREE, to worship and study His Word. If this is you, please call me. Pastor Todd."

Ad in a local paper placed by Reverend Todd, with the hope of moving his congregation from a crowded basement to a larger space, 2002

According to the Lord, the reverend would be able to expand his congregation without paying a cent. The basement he had been preaching in held twenty chairs and nearly thirty people.

"People have called offering places we could rent," Todd said after placing the ad. "That is not what God has told me. The Lord has a building for us that hasn't been used, that someone will be willing to donate."

The Lord, however, neglected to tell that someone the news.

DIVINE CHEESEHEAD

"God told me to sign with the Green Bay Packers."

Reggie White, former NFL defensive star, at his press conference announcing his departure from the Philadelphia Eagles, 1993

White claimed God told him to go to the Packers to sack sin and quarterbacks. Nicknamed the Minister of Defense, the lineman spoke to God often during—and after—his playing career. When he retired, the Lord sat down with him and asked him to reconsider. "God spoke to me and said you made a promise," White said. The promise referred to his contractual obligation to play two more years. "I didn't want to back down on that promise." Not backing down also meant an extra $2.6 million in his pocket.

White preached his beliefs throughout his career, but in the years following his final retirement, he realized pro sports didn't need to be mixed with religion. Just before his death at age forty-three in December 2004, White said, "He doesn't need football to let the world know about Him. When you look at the Scriptures, you'll see that most of the prophets weren't popular guys. I came to the realization that what God needed from me more than anything is a way of living instead of the things I was saying. Now I know I've got to sit down and get it right."

If only that had been the message he spent all those years preaching on the playing field.

ALMIGHTY BED

"God told me it was time to be his wife. Praise be to God I am his wife now."

Sharifat of Nigeria, one of eighty-six wives of a man named Bello, 2008

Sharifat, who was twenty-five when she married her then seventy-four-year-old husband, first met him when she was seeking help for a severe headache. "As soon as I met him the headache was gone," she said. His reputation as a healer led many would-be wives to his ultra king-sized bed.

"I don't go looking for them, they come to me," Bello said. "I will consider the fact that God has asked me to do it and I will just marry them."

Another wife, Ganiat, said after twenty years of marriage: "I am now the happiest woman on earth. When you marry a man with eighty-six wives you know he knows how to look after them."

It is reported that he has at least 170 children, some of whom are older than some of his wives.

Unfortunately for Bello, the BBC brought his story into the limelight, and within weeks, the Nigerian Islamic authority found him in violation of Islamic law (a man is only permitted four wives). Bello agreed to divorce eighty-two wives to avoid facing a death sentence. The good news is he won't be subject to any alimony laws.

SCHOOL BUS

RECKLESS SPIRITUAL JOURNEY

"God told me not to stop [pushing an empty car with my school bus]."

Sharon, two-time "Bus Driver of the Year" winner, on why she pushed a vehicle eight miles before coming to a stop, 1991

Sharon's divine recklessness began when she pulled out of a used-car lot and struck two vehicles, one of which became locked to the front of her bus. At this point, the Lord allegedly encouraged her to keep driving, even with two high school students still aboard. Finally, after eight miles, she shook the car loose with a hard turn and—at God's recommendation—stopped at a mini-mart. Upon emerging from the bus, Sharon offered no explanation to the police, other than the Lord's word. No one was injured.

The award-winning bus driver was an eight-year veteran in the business and had never shown any signs of mental issues or drug abuse. She also served on a countywide bus safety task force. Fortunately for all parties involved, God chose a highly skilled driver to do His bidding.

THE PASSING OF WIND

"I can say with absolute confidence that God did not want me to make that field goal."

John Kasay, Carolina Panthers kicker, on why he missed a forty-seven-yard tying field goal with five seconds left in regulation, 1998

"It was a perfect snap and perfect hold," Kasay explained after the game. "I hit it completely square." Apparently, Kasay believed more in God's desire to interfere in football games than in human error. He had aimed the ball left of the goalposts, anticipating the wind would push the ball to the right and through the uprights. But the wind stopped.

If God was in fact a twelfth defender on the field, He technically should've drawn a penalty flag and forced a re-kick. However, instant replay showed no such foul.

ORIGINAL MATCHMAKER

"The Lord told me to [propose to my sixteen-year-old student]."

Jerry, high school speech teacher, on why he hired a six-foot singing bunny to deliver a written proposal of marriage to the girl's parents, 1992

Jerry had two excellent reasons for choosing an oversized bunny to win over the underage girl's parents: 1) he believed "bunnies are gentle and non-threatening"; and 2) he was a big fan of the 1950 movie *Harvey* featuring a six-foot invisible rabbit. However, in this instance, the bunny was visible and downright creepy.

Just in case hiring a tall, creepy, singing rabbit didn't attract enough attention, the smitten speech coach alerted the media to ensure the whole town knew his feelings—all at the Lord's suggestion. "The more public it is, the more clean it is," Jerry said.

The "relationship" developed when the teacher and student began praying together after class, but Jerry never attempted to touch or see the girl off campus. He simply told her one day that he was in love with her and wanted her to be his wife. (It's evidently what Jerry had been praying for during all those after-school sessions.)

After his proclamation of love and unusual proposal, Jerry once again hired the bunny to deliver roses to the young girl at school, but the fuzzy fellow was denied entrance to the campus. Despite complaints from the girl and her mother, Jerry continued to woo her with an offering of a leather-bound bible and a proposal inscribed within.

Finally, the school principal informed the love-stricken teacher to refrain from any further pursuits because he was acting in an unprofessional manner and was in violation of various board policies. Jerry ignored his boss, answering only to the Big Principal in the sky, and sent an additional card, telegram, and candy with hopes of obtaining a "yes."

HOLY SHIT

"One day, I was scrubbing toilets when the Lord spoke to me clearly: 'Those who want to lead must first learn to serve.'"

Brian, janitor turned entrepreneur, on his inspiration to spread good will through his canine pooper-scooper business, 2006

As the church janitor, Brian was in no position to spread spirituality while cleaning and scrubbing fecal matter. But in founding Disciples on Doody, his dog waste pickup business, Brian brought his passions together by merging ministry with excrement removal—both leading and serving at the same time. As his hands reach toward the ground with a shovel, his voice reaches out to his customers with inspirational words, scripture quotes, and prayers.

DOGGY HEAVEN ON EARTH

"The Lord spoke to me and He said, 'Fifty thousand dollars.'"

Mary, on how much money she would need to care for Cindy, a dog she had raised and then inherited upon the owner's death, 2003

When Mary inherited the seven-year-old cockapoo (a cocker spaniel crossed with a poodle) and $10,000 to care for her, she hired a lawyer to fight for more money from the original owner's heirs, who were left with a $3 million estate.

An actuary claimed the dog had roughly another seven years to live, so Mary prayed to God for guidance as to how much more cash she would need to cover expenses for food, visits to the vet, and, of course, pampering. A preacher conducting a revival at her church helped her hear the Lord's word loud and clear: "The evangelist came to me, looked me dead in the eye, stuck his finger at me, and said, 'Fifty, Sister.'"

"People that has animals, people that loves animals, people that takes care of animals, they'll know I'm not a greedy person," she claimed. "That's not me."

Mary performed her own calculations that evening and generously estimated annual costs of $2,700 in haircuts,

$3,000 in veterinarian bills, $1,000 for food, and $250 for medicine and shampoo. Factoring in $1,500 for gas costs and depreciation of her minivan, she came up with a grand total of $59,150 for the seven years. It turned out God had lowballed her, but Mary stuck with His more conservative estimate.

JOSEPH AND THE BUDGET OF MANY DOLLARS

"The Lord spoke to me, like, out of the blue. You will start a film company. I want you to be the Rolls-Royce of filmmaking. Be better than anyone in the world."

Pastor Richard, on why he set out to create an epic sci-fi blockbuster on the story of Joseph, 2007

Perhaps Steven Spielberg, George Lucas, and James Cameron were simply too busy to make God's film. So He looked to Richard—a San Francisco pastor who had done some local plays and who saw his first movie at the age of forty—to create the world's greatest piece of cinema. Ever.

During an interview on National Public Radio, Richard admitted he found God's choice surprising. "I actually thought Billy Graham. And I was like, dude, man, I am not the guy to do this," he said. Some local church leaders who knew of his small-stage work convinced him God had chosen the right man.

Richard's film, titled *Gravity: The Shadow of Joseph*, tells the biblical character's story from bondage in Egypt to his rise to power. With "an ancient, futuristic" setting, the story is described as a cross between *Star Wars* and *The Ten Commandments* and is budgeted at $200 million.

The pastor created his own production company, cast the roles, had costumes and sets designed, and began shooting in a rustic little town in Italy. But despite Richard's tremendous efforts on such a massive undertaking, the masterpiece remains unfinished. In the meantime, God is microwaving an omnipresent bowl of popcorn.

ROAD WRATH

"The Lord told me not to stop [barreling down the highway in a tractor-trailer]."

Leroy, trucker, on why he led police on a high-speed chase through three counties in Tennessee, 2001

Three bullets into one of Leroy's tires disagreed with the Lord and finally brought the big rig to a stop—but not before it ran a dozen motorists off the road.

The Lord's work began early in the morning when Leroy ran through a roadblock. The lieutenant who fired the shots described his first sight of the tractor-trailer: "It was just like a train, going full force at 70 mph with the horn blaring. Like he was on a mission."

Once apprehended, Leroy confirmed the officer's theory by explaining that God had egged him on. However, the Lord had not acted alone. "The Mad Hatter made me do it," the crazed trucker also told the lieutenant.

Amazingly, no one was hurt in the ordeal. Leroy was charged with two counts of vehicular assault, evading arrest, and reckless endangerment. And for His role, God was thanked by those who safely escaped harm.

HOCKING HOLY MATRIMONY

"God spoke to me and said, 'Maybe a wedding chapel will be a good thing to put in that pawnshop.'"

Ted, Houston pawnshop owner, on the answer to his wedding ring surplus problem, 1993

Tough economic times in the early '80s led to Ted's pawnshop collecting more rings than it could handle. He didn't have the heart to melt them down, but fortunately, the Lord stepped in with His innovative chapel idea. Ordained through the mail by the National Chaplains Association, Ted built the chapel in the back of his pawnshop, with a miniature façade, including fake stained glass windows and Christmas lights blinking around the structure's frame.

"This is the only place in town you can get married and buy a gun all at the same time," Ted said during an interview on National Public Radio. A shotgun wedding couldn't be easier.

The pawnshop advertised its services with a "Buy a ring, get a free wedding" offer. But accessories are extra. A wedding dress rental costs $20, a bouquet of flowers, $14.95, and, if desired, the organ played during the ceremony can be purchased for just $200. A Polaroid of the newlyweds is, however, complimentary.

In the late 1990s, Ted expanded his get-married-quick-and-cheap niche by offering even greater speed and convenience with a pioneering drive-thru chapel. An old, rickety, converted guard shack behind the shop allowed couples to simply roll down the window and say "I do."

THOU SHALT ALMOST WIN

"God said, 'Stand up, dry your tears and tell your teammates that next year you're going back to the championship game.'"

Bubba Paris, former NFL offensive lineman for the San Francisco 49ers, telling his teammates the good news after losing the NFC Championship Game to the New York Giants, 1990

Bubba Paris had misinterpreted the message from God. The team wasn't going back to the championship; he was. During the off-season Paris moved from the 49ers to the woeful Indianapolis Colts, which he assumed was championship-bound. After a 1–12 start, the team cut him, freeing players from hearing Paris talk about their glorious destiny despite the dismal record. The Detroit Lions picked up Paris and did in fact make it to the NFC Championship Game in 1991 but lost to the Washington Redskins.

God loved Bubba but apparently not enough to win the big one.

SUPREME OOPS

"God told me to go and kill. So I got my pistol and shot him."

Lorenza, aka "Shootie," on why he fatally shot a man four times, 1937

Beyond getting the nod from God, Lorenza justified his actions as a form of revenge. He claimed the victim had once "given me some poison whiskey with snakes in it. Ever since then I have had snakes in my stomach. This morning I was sweeping around my door—suddenly he put the jinks on me." That's when God allegedly came in to settle the dispute.

The victim, Willie, told police before dying in the hospital that he'd never met "Shootie" and believed it was a case of mistaken identity.

TRUCK STOPPER

"The Lord spoke to me and said to give everything away. I said, 'Surely, Lord, you don't mean everything?' But He did...That first year was pretty rough."

Bunny, trucker for Jesus, recounting the call that led him to hit the road with his eighteen-wheel mobile chapel, 1983

It was eight years earlier that Bunny, along with his wife, Blonnie, heeded the Lord's command and sold everything—except a few necessities—to purchase their Ford truck. With the words "Trucking for Jesus" plastered diagonally across the side of the eighteen-wheeler, the Virginia-based couple began making annual rounds to 1,500 truck stops across America, spreading the good word to truckers everywhere. Six wooden pews formed the chapel in the back of the Ford, where Bunny and Blonnie played the banjo and guitar as they preached.

Because truckers and God are up at all hours, the chapel remained open 24 hours a day, 365 days a year. "Our motto is: 'We doze, but we never close,'" Bunny said. And if the giant "Trucking for Jesus" didn't catch a driver's attention at three o'clock in the morning, his CB handle surely would: "I'm Virginia's No. 1 double-clutchin' trailer-truckin' fried-chicken-lickin' preacherman."

Altogether, it was a big 10-4 to the Lord.

YEE HAW-LLELUJAH

"I was standing out here praying about the cowboy church idea one day, and the Lord told me just to use whatever I've got."

Preston, on how he started his own North Carolina church on horses, 2009

The idea to form the Cowboy Church came to Preston out of necessity: "When you work five days a week, and have to take care of your horse on Saturday, Sunday is the only day left to ride them. Then you have to choose between going to church and riding your horse."

Not with the Cowboy Church.

"We're just offering a choice where you can go to church and ride your horse at the same time," he says.

Members participate in a service under a large tarp next to a horse pen, where the four-legged members anxiously await a ride. The cowboys sing, pray, preach, and make donations in a cowboy hat, as opposed to the traditional offering plate. Of course, tradition is miles from the pasture. Typical attire at Cowboy Church includes jeans (held up with giant belt buckles), cowboy boots, and western hats. "This is the only church you can come to where, if you have horse manure on your pants, we won't complain," Preston says.

If the idea catches on, it's only a matter of time before other entrepreneurs talk to God about conveniently merging recreation with worship. Football Church, anyone?

GOD FRAUD

"The Lord spoke to me and said, 'It's not flesh and blood that are fighting. It's me and the devil and I'm going to win!'"

Tammy Faye Bakker, discussing her husband's upcoming fraud and conspiracy trial on the *Jim and Tammy Show*, 1989

In their heyday, televangelists Jim and Tammy Faye Bakker raised more than $100 million annually through their popular show, *The P.T.L.* (Praise The Lord) *Club*. When the Lord told Jim that He wanted the Bakkers to build a Christian resort, the preacher solicited $158 million in donations and built Heritage USA in Fort Mill, South Carolina—complete with a luxury hotel, a water park, playgrounds, tennis courts, canoeing, and shopping galore. However, Bakker had sold tens of thousands of "lifetime memberships" offering annual three-night stays at the hotel, and with only five hundred rooms, he had no means to accommodate the memberships.

By the mid-1980s, a financial crisis struck the resort and hundreds were laid off between Thanksgiving and Christmas of 1985. Yet, despite the job cuts and lack of accommodations, Bakker was giving himself a $3.1 million bonus and using the ministry's money to indulge in personal luxuries, including a Rolls-Royce and gold-plated bathroom fixtures. In 1987, an additional $279,000 was spent in an effort to suppress Bakker's affair with Jessica Hahn, a former church secretary. If the Lord was battling the devil, the flesh was getting in on the action.

By 1988, Bakker's financial woes led to charges of fraud and conspiracy. "I was doing my best to run the ministry on a budget," Bakker testified. The jury felt his best wasn't good enough, finding him guilty on twenty-four counts. He was sentenced to forty-five years in federal prison but ultimately served only five years.

Tammy Faye divorced Jim Bakker in 1992. Twelve years later, her fame landed her a spot on VH1's *The Surreal Life*, where she got to hang out with porn star Ron Jeremy and Vanilla Ice.

LET THERE BE MILLIONS

"God told me [to accept nothing less than $5 million a year, four years, guaranteed]."

Sean Gilbert, NFL defensive tackle, on why he refused to sign with the Washington Redskins, opting instead to sit out the entire 1997 season

Having an all-knowing, all-powerful being for an agent proved quite valuable to Gilbert. Sure, fans were angered after he turned down an offer of $3.6 million, left the team without a defensive anchor, and held out for the season. But the following year, the Carolina Panthers signed him to a seven-year, $47.5 million contract. More than twice what he was demanding of the Redskins.

All that big money helped the Panthers finish with a 4–12 record in 1998. And God reminded us that even losers can be winners.

BIG BANG II

"God has wanted me to [blow up a hotel] for a long time and tonight I finally had the courage. I have never had any peace."

John, factory worker and former coal miner, in a note left explaining why he set off three dynamite explosions in a suburban Detroit hotel, 1954

John finally granted God's wish—although it cost him his life, sent five others to the hospital, and left the hotel with a gaping hole twenty-five feet high and fifteen feet wide. The deranged factory worker once lived in that very hotel until unusual behavior, such as setting his room afire, forced the manager to kick him out.

One of the victims told police he knew John and had seen the dynamite in his room: "[John] said he was going to get even—that he had to get his revenge. He said, 'The good Lord told me I've got to kill somebody.'" Unfortunately for John, God failed to inform him who that somebody would be.

RETURNS MESSIAH

"God told me in a dream how to get tax refunds."

Mary, welfare recipient turned fraudulent tax preparer, on what she told her clients, 1973

The low-income entrepreneur was indicted by a federal grand jury, along with nine others, on charges of tax return fraud. Only one of her cohorts was an actual accountant; among the other defendants was a retired employee of the Atlantic City tax division, a part-time security guard, and a real estate agent.

Together, the group inflated their clients' numbers wherever possible, from medical and dental expenses to charitable deductions. In some cases, they even deducted gasoline taxes for clients who didn't own a vehicle. Clients were each guaranteed a refund, with the defendants earning a percentage.

By using exaggerated numbers, Mary and her accomplices earned their customers large refunds when they were due either smaller refunds or nothing at all. Unfortunately, what started off as a dream turned into a legal nightmare.

MOTHER MARY JANE

"The Creator has instructed me [to grow pot]."

Lawrence, self-proclaimed Soto Nation spiritual chief, defending himself in court on charges of production and possession of marijuana for the purpose of trafficking, Saskatchewan, 2008

Naturally, the pot was being grown for medicinal purposes. Good intentions aside, six thousand marijuana plants, potentially worth $5 million, were seized in a drug raid.

Lawrence, also known by his Indian name, Kitchi O-Stew Ka-Nee-Ka-Na-Go-Shick Ogimow-Wacon Ka-Nee-Ka-Neet ("the one who always walks first"), was one of six defendants and claimed to be growing the marijuana plants to help cure diabetes—at the Lord's command. "You know, when the Creator tells me I must do something, I have absolutely no choice," he explained.

During the trial, the spiritual chief clutched a sacred bundle holding a pipe that had been passed down from his ancestors. He described this bundle as a "telephone to the Creator." God, however, did not call in to testify in his defense.

Lawrence was sentenced to six years in prison.

LORD 1, LANDLORD 0

"God told me to take care of [fifty dogs]. I'm not going to abandon them."

Reverend A. Gail of the Sacred Church of Life, on why she refused to leave her home, 1997

While fifty dogs are no landlord's dream, his real beef was in regards to the $15,000 the reverend owed in rent for her three trailers on the half-acre, garbage-strewn lot. Yet, because of the dogs, he was unable to evict her—a law prohibits officials from making animals homeless when enforcing a court order, meaning they must first find shelter for the pooches.

"My life has been pure hell for the last year," the landlord said. "I have tried to abide by the law and settle the matter through the courts. But I'm being penalized by everybody along the way."

God may have told the reverend to care for the dogs, but clearly, the dogs were taking care of her.

HOLY
BIBLE

BLESSED BRIBERY

"God told me to pay white folks."

Bishop Fred, on his attempt to create a multicultural congregation by paying white people $5 to attend a service at his all-black Louisiana church, 2004

The Lord had good intentions, but after the novelty of scoring five bucks for exploring a black church wore off, the white folks stopped attending.

"They came from as far away as London and Dallas-Fort Worth," the bishop boasted. "A lot of white people came, and they went back to their white holes. Because I'll say it again: 11 a.m. on Sunday morning is the most segregated hour in America."

God wanted less talk and more action. In addition to the month-long $5 gimmick, Fred offered a more lucrative $10 to whites visiting the obscure Thursday night service.

The offer, however, was very strict in accordance with God's words. A few American Indians attempted to cash in but were denied the cash because "they were Indians, not white folks." Fred claimed he didn't want to be hustled.

Once the promotion was over, attendance returned to its status quo. "And God," the bishop said, "is angry with us."

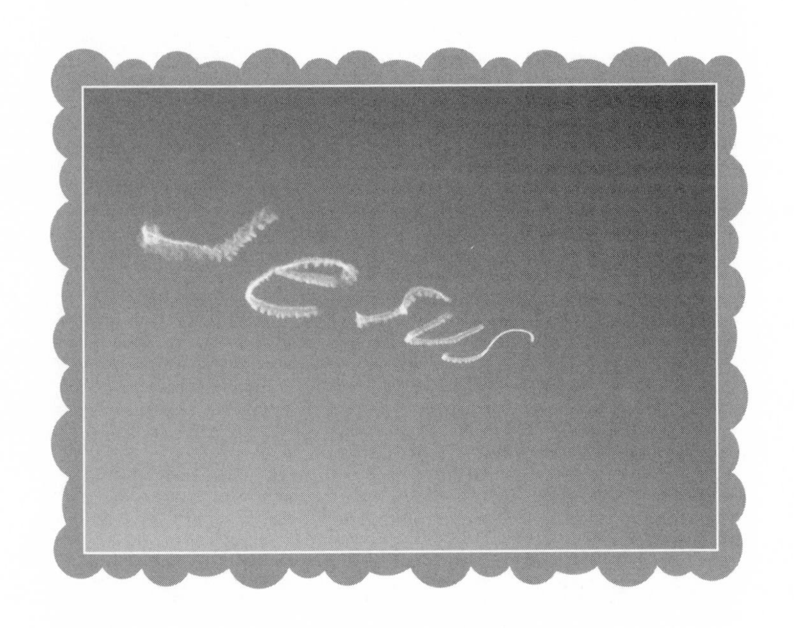

THE WRITING ON THE SKY

"Jesus told me to move to Orlando. God told me to [skywrite]. I'm just a ballpoint pen, spreading the word."

Jerry, skywriter, on why he regularly posts spiritual messages high in the sky, 2007

Look up toward heaven from the theme parks of Orlando, and the Lord's word may be waiting for you—courtesy of His own private skywriter. Piloting a yellow Grumman Agcat crop duster, nicknamed Holy Smoke, Jerry has spent eight years posting what he calls "love letters from God." His "ballpoint pen" has written such messages as "God loves you" and "Jesus loves you" 10,000 feet in the air across God's vast stationery.

But these love letters haven't always been received as such. On New Year's Day 2002, Jerry posted the boastful "God is Great" message in the skies of Boca Raton, not far from where several of the September 11th terrorists lived and trained. It was also the site of the first anthrax attack. Frightened residents flooded the authorities and newspapers with calls believing the skywriter was related to another terrorist plot.

God may be great, but in this case, His timing wasn't.

DEAR LORD

"The Lord told me what to do...I went immediately to my son's room and tore up those disgusting photos. I felt like a ten-ton weight had been lifted from my shoulders. At least I am sure now that no one else will ever see those filthy pictures."

"Waiting and Worrying," in her second letter to Ann Landers regarding nudie pictures found under her twenty-one-year-old son's mattress, 1980

In her first letter to the famed advice columnist, signed "Shocked Mom," she spoke of finding nude photos of her son and his girlfriend, most of which featured obscene poses. "Shocked Mom" explained that her son was "always a decent, moral person" who "never got mixed up with dope or alcohol like the children of some of our friends." Her illusion was shattered after changing his bed sheets and discovering the naughty pictures. "I was very proud of him until today," she wrote.

But rather than wait patiently for Landers's response, she sought God's advice and got a speedy answer. Unfortunately, obeying His recommendation simply created more problems, so "Shocked Mom" wrote back as "Waiting and Worrying" and asked what to do when her son found his photos missing. This time, she heard from Landers: "Those pictures belonged to your son. You had no business tearing them up." Landers advised the shocked and worried mom to keep quiet and to reveal the truth if asked and inadvertently reminded readers why she—not God—was the one with the syndicated newspaper column.

BROKEN PROMISES

"The voice of God said 'Be ready! Prepare! You will die at seven o'clock on Sunday morning, June 14.' Then He disappeared."

Anna, survivor of God's death sentence, 1908

Upon making her prediction public, Anna was placed under hospital care. Doctors determined that unless she committed suicide, there was no reason she would suddenly expire on the designated date. "They don't believe I will die at the hour named, but I know I will, for God told me so," Anna told reporters. She awoke that morning "as plump and robust" as she was prior to hearing the bad news.

Once again, God disappeared on her.

UNTAKEN SACRED VOWS

"You see, I had a vision, and the Lord told me to go to Washington. He showed me that I was to marry Ethel Roosevelt. She is the President's daughter, and the Lord has willed that we marry."

Thaddeus, Kentucky grocer, explaining his need for funds to continue his journey to the Capitol, 1906

Thaddeus trekked from Lexington to Cincinnati before his cash dried up. Determined to carry on, he visited the local police station and asked the chief to help with his transportation needs, fully explaining his calling from God. But the Lord hadn't reckoned on facing the acumen of a local Ohio lawman. Rather than comply, the chief thwarted Thaddeus's mission by giving him a cell to spend the night in and seeking out the hopeful First Son-in-Law's family for help.

Ethel Roosevelt, who was only fifteen years old at the time, eventually married a doctor instead. Thaddeus made no attempts to crash the wedding.

SOYLENT GOD

"I don't regret it, my conscience is clear. God told me I was to punish people. I think I will keep on killing and eating."

Ozgur, on his arrest for the murder and consumption of a fifty-five-year-old man, Turkey, 2007

The twenty-seven-year-old murderer calmly explained to his arresting officers that he had an irresistible urge to eat people, and that in this case he had intentionally gone to the park to kill someone. Armed with a gun and a "special knife," he struck up a conversation with the victim on a bench. Then he simply stood up, walked behind the man, and shot him twice before dragging him off to his car like a proud hunter.

"I cut off some meat with a cleaver," Ozgur said. "Then I felt [nauseated], so I ate some of it raw to get over that and put the rest in my bag. I found I liked the taste." He put the leftovers in the fridge at home, where his parents also lived.

A few months prior to the murder, he shot another man in the head and stomach, but the victim miraculously escaped. "If he hadn't gotten away I would have cut him up too. I murder because I want to eat human flesh," Ozgur claimed.

If God had any excuse in this case, it might be that He has a twisted sense of humor: The Turkish word for "cannibal" is "yamyam," which is pronounced "yum yum."

LEADED
GAS

INFERNAL AFFAIR

"God told me to burn down a church."

Unidentified woman arrested shortly after telling a handyman her plans for the three cans of gasoline he helped her fill at three o'clock in the morning, 1996

Working in mysterious ways is one thing, but God is flat out sending mixed signals in this case.

Fortunately for the church, the handyman was a little curious about the sudden need for gasoline in the wee hours of the morning. He promptly called the police after hearing the explanation. Still, the sacrilegious woman almost followed through with her plan—before the arrest was made, she had gone as far as pouring gasoline under one of the church doors. A patrolman spotted the canisters outside the church before any fire had been lit, and the catastrophe was averted.

"I guess God was watching out for us," the church deacon said.

NO RAM THIS TIME

"God told me to do it...I know God can do anything. He can move mountains. He could stop that bullet in the air. In the Bible God stopped Abraham from killing his son. In my heart, I thought the bullets would be duds."

Richard, at his sanity hearing for the murder of his invalid mother, 1956

According to the religious twenty-three-year-old, a series of prayers led to an unorthodox conversation with God.

Rather than speaking directly to the Lord, Richard told the sanity commission that he wrote the word "yes" on one side of a paper and tossed it in the air. As it tumbled to the ground, he repeated names to himself, ending with his mother's when the paper landed yes-side-up. Next, he asked the paper if he should kill her. Again, he gave it a toss, and it answered in the affirmative. Richard was conflicted. He knew one of the Ten Commandments said killing was off limits, so to clarify the "Lord's will," he positioned his fingers in the shape of a gun, looked in the mirror, and said, "You mean 'bang, bang' like this?" The paper said yes.

Armed with a rifle (he kept one in the house for shooting rats), Richard was fully prepared to obey the holy paper. Three shots killed his mother, who suffered from Parkinson's disease, as she sat in her wheelchair watching television.

Richard had cared for his mother for years and explained to the commission, "I loved my mother more than any person on this earth. But it came down to 'Who do you love more, God or your mother?'"

Sadly, no angel appeared before Richard with a last-second sacrificial beast—even with all those house rats running around.

BAD LUCK CAT

"One of the people [God told me was] in hell was my girlfriend, Stacey. God told me that Stacey was going to destroy me. God also told me that I had to take Stacey's cat. He told me that the cat was evil."

Albert, explaining to police his reasons for killing his girlfriend and her cat, 1984

Albert is an example of someone who had way too many conversations with God.

He and his girlfriend, Stacey, had been living together for

nearly ten years when God stepped into the relationship and mucked everything up. Suddenly, Albert was convinced that Stacey was hitting the bars, having an affair, and slipping drugs into his food. "God told me that if I could get Stacey to admit what she was doing that He could forgive her." But attempts to make her confess failed, and he felt God urging him to kill her.

"God kept telling me to do it. God told me to dispose of Stacey. God told me if I didn't dispose of her she was just gonna keep on. I started to cry because of what God had told me." The Lord also allegedly threatened to "destroy" Stacey and her little cat too on His own if Albert couldn't handle it. The conflicted boyfriend wanted to run away from his dilemma and ignore God's command: "I tried leaving, but I was prevented from doing that because I got in an accident with my car and I couldn't leave." God's plan was not to be avoided.

Finally, Albert armed himself with an extension cord and succumbed to the horrifying mission. "I decided to do what Moses did to one of the pharaohs," he said. "I decided to strangle Stacey." As if being strangled to death by her boyfriend wasn't bad enough, God added insult to injury by saying, "When Stacey died, He would make sure she burned in hell."

The couple's cat was next. "Stacey's cat watched me strangle Stacey. I knew the cat was evil. After I finished with Stacey, I went to the kitchen and destroyed the cat."

With the job done, Albert did the right thing and flagged down a sheriff's car passing by outside.

A judge declared him "dangerously mentally ill" and committed him to a secure mental health facility.

SPEED
LIMIT
55

RIGHTEOUS ROAD TRIP

"While going through your state on vacation, I exceeded the speed limit at one place so the Lord has told me to pay the state $17.50."

Letter to the West Virginia state police from a Maryland motorist, 1962

Because God failed to fill out the proper paperwork, there was no record of a violation, and the money was returned to the devout speed demon.

BAD BEGETS EVIL

"God told me to [bludgeon them] because they were bad."

Gabriel, on why he murdered his parents, brother, and sister, 1962

In his police statement, the twenty-six-year-old murderer offered greater detail on his family's badness: his parents had once been in an argument with some other people; his thirty-six-year-old sister had no job; and, worst of all, his twenty-eight-year-old brother didn't clean the eggs produced on the family farm.

While being held by authorities, doctors examined self-inflicted gashes around Gabriel's eyes—a much less severe punishment for being really, really bad.

LACK OF JUDGMENT DAY

"God told me to leave Princeton."

Najib, Princeton University senior and head of a fundamentalist student group called the "Church at Princeton," on why he dropped out of school before graduation, 1982

According to God, a summer apocalypse was headed straight for the Ivy League school because it encouraged sin. No specific sin was cited, but the Lord convinced Najib that dropping out of the prestigious university was the best thing for his future. He fled for safety and prepared to watch all those diploma-waving sinners perish.

"There's going to be an awesome judgment," the young church leader said. "The university has been corrupted from what it was originally intended to be."

Like Najib, God failed to display any awesome judgment.

MESSIAH LIBIDO

"One day I was in my trailer just relaxing and there was nothing on my mind in particular and then God said to me you are the Messiah."

Michael, leader of a fifty-six-member New Mexico cult, recalling the moment he began to fulfill his destiny, 2008

The Messiah is here. And after thousands of years, boy is he horny.

Following in the grand tradition of David Koresh and Jim Jones, sixty-six-year-old Michael's status as cult head honcho meant God wanted him to have lots of sex with whatever females followed him, whether they were married or not. This included his son's wife. All cuckolds were told that consummation with the Messiah was God's command, and if they didn't like it, they could scream, shake a fist, or flip the bird directly at Him.

Even underage virgins got in on the action. Michael claimed to have had seven naked girls in bed but abstained from sex, despite one of the virgins threatening suicide if he didn't do the deflowering honors.

In a National Geographic documentary, one of Michael's followers described her sexual encounter: "He took me to bed and laid me down and somehow it was like all of heaven was open to me, somehow I started to see God, after all he is the Son of God."

However, the cult leader expected his carnal delights to be short-lived since he predicted Judgment Day would arrive on October 31, 2007. When the world survived Halloween, Michael proved even messiahs can make mistakes. Regardless, his followers stayed at his side and patiently awaited their time to ascend to the next world.

Six months later, state police arrested the Messiah on three charges of criminal sexual contact.

NOAH JR.

"I told him, 'I know you said you'd never sell another inch of your land. But God told me to ask you if you would donate another acre to Him for the ark.'"

Reverend Richard, on how he got a stubborn farmer to sell him a fourth acre of land to create space for his 450-foot replica of Noah's ark, 1977

The quest for the ark began with a series of nightly visions after Richard's small church purchased the initial three acres as part of an expansion plan. For three months, he saw Noah preaching to sinners and building an ark. "It was as real, as clear to me as I see you sitting there," Richard once explained to a visitor. Shortly after, while browsing in a Christian bookstore, he opened a book to a page featuring a drawing of what Noah's ark may have looked like—and exactly like what he saw in his visions. That coincidence clinched it.

Members of the congregation approved the project—a great miracle in Richard's eyes. Just a few years before, they had rejected a plan to spend $2,000 on new pews and lights.

Not only would building the ark help Richard fulfill an end-of-days biblical prophecy in Matthew 24:37 ("But as the days of Noah were, so shall also the coming of the Son of Man be."), but its location on U.S. Route 48 would qualify it as a roadside attraction. "People who wouldn't be caught dead in a church—out of curiosity they'll come to see what Noah's ark was like and we'll share Christ with them," Richard reasoned.

When it became clear that three acres of land was insufficient for his massive ark, Richard paid the old, obstinate farmer another visit. God gave the pastor the appropriate words of persuasion, and sure enough, the landowner changed his mind.

NOAH III

"Before I pounded the first nail, I was ready to quit. I looked at the enormity of [building an ark] and felt overwhelmed with the logistics, the questions, the doubts. But God told me to get up today and pound a nail. Don't worry about tomorrow."

Peter, Baptist minister and veteran shipbuilder, on the ark he planned to build and sail to Haiti, 1994

Peter pounded more than 25,000 nails into 850 beams and 400 sheets of plywood over a fifteen-month period. And where nails couldn't be pounded, 260 gallons of epoxy worked its adhesive magic.

Unlike Noah, Peter had no intention of filling his ninety-three-foot ark with animal couplets. Instead, God asked him to sail from the Florida Keys to Haiti, delivering food, household goods, and the gospel. Peter planned to sail to and fro, offering goods on a regular basis.

Funding the Almighty's command proved to be its own challenge. Peter pulled an initial $40,000 from his savings and donations and wished to sell his home and relocate his wife and seven children to the fully furnished ark. Altogether, he hoped $90,000 would cover the costs of the vessel.

A noble mission, but how many supplies could all that money have bought if God told Peter to use FedEx instead?

BLOW WORSHIP

"The Lord told me to tell you and to tell our city you don't have to worry because you've already won...don't worry about Judge Jackson and don't worry about the jury."

Bishop Clarence, addressing Washington DC mayor Marion Barry, who was on trial for cocaine and perjury charges, 1990

If "winning" is spending six months in jail, then the Lord spoke the truth.

The crack-smoking mayor faced charges of cocaine possession after an FBI sting led to his arrest in a DC hotel. Unbeknownst to him, the female friend he'd been partying with was working with agents in the investigation. Barry offered these words to his constituents: "The bitch set me up."

However, the bishop may have been prophesizing Barry's victory four years later, when he won his fourth term in the 1994 mayoral election.

EXODUS FROM THE LAND OF FLORIDA

"We've left behind business, good homes, everything. If it wasn't for the prophecy, we wouldn't be here. God told us to leave Miami."

Reverend Norka, on her congregation's exodus from Miami after a Guatemalan woman had a vision of a tidal wave devastating Florida, 1976

All two hundred fearful members of Reverend Norka's congregation fled Miami based on the Guatemalan's prediction, which she claimed would occur in just a few short months. The alleged prophet previously had a vision of an earthquake in Guatemala four months before it happened.

Despite her earlier accuracy, scientists disagreed with the Guatemalan soothsayer. "The chances of a major tidal wave in the Atlantic Ocean is essentially nil," said a representative of Miami's National Oceanic and Atmospheric Administration.

Norka's followers weren't about to take any chances on science. One member packed three twenty-gallon trash containers of carburetors with the intent of starting an auto repair business in Tennessee. "We have no plans to return to Florida," the fleeing entrepreneur said. "We wouldn't return, not even to count $100 bills if they were offered. While counting, the wave could take us away." And they most certainly did not return for retirement.

THOU SHALT GET FREAKY

"God told us to open a sex shop."

Stan and Stella, on why they decided to open an online Christian XXX boutique, 2006

The sex business has flourished ever since God was just a wee deity creating raging hormones in man and woman. This is His attempt to do it with values.

"Sex has that forbidden, dirty image but sex in marriage is God's idea and it's great," said Stella. "It's all based on sex within a marriage and we offer advice, discussion and the shop."

So as not to offend God or God-fearing shoppers, the clean sex shop does not offer any bondage items, shows no pornography, and all lingerie models are headless.

The couple received the support of their local church leaders and has garnered positive response from the majority of the ten thousand daily visitors. Of course, there are those who believe they never had such conversations with God: "We have had people telling us we are working for Satan and we are going to hell," Stella admitted.

HOLY MOLE MEN

"The Lord told us through prophecy that soon there will be devastation on earth and one-third of all the people will be destroyed."

Letter to a friend from a member of the Full Gospel Assembly religious cult, 1960

It was a time when world peace seemed fragile and a Russian atomic attack appeared imminent. Anticipating the worst, 120 members of the Full Gospel Assembly decided to simply vanish until the turmoil passed.

The disappearing act began with a move to the small town of Benson, Arizona, where the group swiftly erected homes and a small church, painting a picture of normalcy to the surrounding neighbors. But the cultists were secretly stocking up on groceries and digging furiously. Heeding the prophecy of leader Sister Ann, they burrowed their way through closet floors to seek shelter underground, beneath multiple trap doors. They planned to resurface after the destruction to win the world's leftovers for the Lord.

Several weeks into hiding, a handful of members defied God's warning and left their shelters early. Two were arrested on charges of kidnapping, accused by angry fathers of "secreting their children in underground bomb shelters." While the complainants were not members of the cult, their wives were and had remained huddled underground with their children. "If you hear a rumble and a roar, we'd appreciate being rushed back to the shelter," one of the prisoners told an officer from his jail cell. "We are all waiting for a sign from Him telling us when to come out," he added.

Forty-two days later, the entire group emerged to face the sun and the still-intact outside world once again. "God was putting us through a test," Sister Ann said. "The real thing will happen another time in the not too distant future." Some members dipped back into their underground holes over the next several years but popped back up after just a few days, saddened by the complete and utter lack of bombing.

By the end of the decade, a minister in the movement grew tired of Sister Ann's insistence that devastation was just around the corner and split off from the group, along with half its members. "She was a good woman at first," he said of Ann. "But then she started using witchcraft, black magic, hypnotism. She brainwashes her followers."

The split caused anger throughout the settlement, with both sides bickering over the upcoming obliteration of the human race and barricading each other's streets. "There's bitterness and rancor everywhere in this tiny colony," the minister said.

God brought destruction to Benson—but without an atomic bomb.

BLESSED AGORAPHOBIA, PART 1

"This [motel] is where God told us to go, and this is where we'll stay until God tells us to leave or man forces us out."

Sister Esther, cult member, on why she and three other cultists refused to leave a small motel room stripped of beds, water, and power, 1983

Led by a former pimp, the obedient foursome lived in the ten-foot-by-ten-foot room for six months without paying a dime. Management pulled the basic comforts from the modest dwelling after three months, yet the group wouldn't budge. Prayer and assistance from friends helped them through their self-imposed difficult times.

When the Lord first instructed the small cult to huddle up inside the motel, they had the luxury of welfare to pay the rent. Once it came time to reapply for benefits, no one left the room and the money ran dry. "God wanted to show us the system was no good," the ex-pimp explained.

A court-appointed eviction order finally allowed the system to have the last say as authorities dragged the group from their barren abode.

BLESSED AGORAPHOBIA, PART 2

"God told us to [stay in jail]."

Religious cultists, shortly after being forced out of the empty motel room God told them to stay in, 1984

It didn't take long for the cultists to receive new instructions from above after their motel room debacle [see Blessed Agoraphobia, Part 1]. Considering they had no electricity, water, or beds at their prior digs, prison was a step up.

The group of three discovered the joys of jail when its members were arrested for violating a park curfew in a small Connecticut town. They were released, but they returned to the police headquarters hours later seeking shelter, explaining that it was the Lord's will. They further explained that they are "vessels of God, the only true believers," and that the East Coast is doomed unless everyone else repents for their sins.

The police chief allowed them to stay in jail, giving them freedom to come and go as they wished, but the group preferred to treat themselves like prisoners and made no efforts to find a more suitable living space. After two days, it became clear they had sentenced themselves to a long stay, so the chief took it upon himself to overrule God and issued an eviction. "Being that the group has made no effort on their own in their brief stay to seek help from anyone, the department no longer feels obliged to provide shelter," he said.

A psychiatrist examining the group determined they were competent, thereby ruling out a cozy stay at a mental institution.

20
40
60
80
100
120
140
160
MPH
0
1
2
3
4
5

PICKUP TAKEDOWN

"[She] was not driving like a Christian. God said...she needed to be taken off the road."

Michael, telling deputies why he rammed into another driver at 100 miles per hour, 2008

The fifty-two-year-old Texan floored his pickup at the Lord's behest, explaining to authorities "It was Jesus' will for him to punish the car." Yet, neither Michael nor Jesus offered any details on what sorts of vehicular sins the victim committed.

Fortunately, the punishment was not as severe as it could have been—both vehicles spun across a median before coming to a stop, but neither driver was injured and no other cars were involved.

"God must have been with them," said the local lieutenant, apparently agreeing with Michael's claim. "'Cause any other time, the severity of this crash, it would have been fatal."

Michael's defense may prove a bit shakier when facing his charges of aggravated assault with a deadly weapon.

THE DIVINE RIGHT TO BEAR ARMS

"The Lord told me to give you my Belgium Browning Sweet Sixteen shotgun."

Unidentified hunter speaking to Jim, an ordained minister and host of the syndicated show, *God's Great Outdoors*, 2002

When the unknown man offered the weapon to Jim at a Louisiana Sportsman Banquet, the surprised minister asked, "Are you sure He told you that?" The man answered yes: "I never use it, but I know you will."

By placing the shotgun in Jim's possession, God saw to it that it could never *not* do any harm again. The hunting minister immediately bought a box of 16-gauge shells and killed twelve doves—none of which were carrying an olive branch.

DOOM AND PRISON GLOOM

"They are a stubborn and rebellious people, ignoring the voice of the Lord. I will destroy them."

Patricia, delivering the Lord's prophecy in regards to the small town of Erie, Kansas (population 1,296), 1962

The sixteen-year-old prophet scared the bejeezus out of her entire family with a series of doom-and-gloom prophecies. Her parents spread the fear with letters mailed to the townsfolk, warning them of the upcoming wrath.

"Take a few belongings and have them ready, for you must flee quickly," Patricia said in a follow-up prophecy. "Go in cars, and have them ready at the door."

Patricia's father, Kenneth, quickly made preparations to do just as God commanded, but in pulling the youngest two of his six children out of school, he landed himself in jail. A state law required children to attend school until the age of sixteen or until graduating the eighth grade—whichever comes first apparently.

With their plans gone awry, the rest of the clan—Mom, Grandma, and all the little ones—packed up their two cars, parked them outside the jail, and lived in them while they awaited Kenneth's freedom. Chants of "Stop them! O Lord, stop them!" offered no help.

Kenneth explained to the judge that he couldn't return his children to school because it "is out of my hands. I have been commanded by God and dare not disobey." When a reporter asked how he could relocate his family from behind bars, Kenneth simply said: "God will deliver me."

Erie still exists today, with the population remaining essentially the same as it was nearly fifty years ago. No further reports offered information on Kenneth's release from jail.

THE ROOFS ARE ON FIRE

"God told us to [burn fifty-three of our homes]."

Statement from members of the Canadian Radical Sons of Freedom
Doukhobors cult, 1962

Demonstrating just a touch of good sense, the Freedomites removed all their belongings from their homes before setting them aflame. Some watched the infernos quietly as they tended to their nearby gardens. Others stripped their clothes off and threw rocks and water at police and reporters.

Fortunately, no taxpayer dollars were wasted, as the Freedomite community had no fire department.

The newly homeless cultists offered no explanation other than divine instruction but had traditionally burned and bombed property to protest government intervention in their matters. Just a few years earlier, thirty-seven Doukhobor women set fire to their prison barracks, saying God told them to do it in protest of the coming of World War III.

LOUIS THE APOSTLE

"God commanded me to [set the earth on fire]."

Louis, on why he set off a small explosion in the back room of a Brooklyn bar, 1900

At the sound of the sudden explosion, Michael the bartender rushed to the back room and discovered a fire and Louis dancing joyfully around it. The arsonist invited Michael to boogie around the flames with him. He declined, choosing instead to thrust Louis out of the way and extinguish the fire. Not only did he foil the Lord's dastardly plan, but he potentially saved the planet and all of mankind.

Louis, however, wasn't ready to give up on his mission. He told authorities he would never be taken alive because he was one of the Lord's twelve apostles and he was sent to earth with specific instructions to burn it. Nevertheless, the arsonist was subdued and brought to the courthouse. His divine-inspired defense compelled the judge to postpone the case until Louis's sanity was examined. "No you don't," he responded. "Don't you put this case off at all. It must go on right away, and you must give me money."

No explanations were offered for the time sensitivity of the case or the sudden request for funds. The Lord's apostle proceeded to curse at the courtroom, throw his hat at a lawyer, and struggle with three officers as they returned him to his cell.

ADD A PINCH OF GOD

"God came to me in a dream and gave me this sauce."

John, aka "Big Daddy," owner of the Dreamland rib shack, explaining the source of his recipe to editors of a barbecue sauce cookbook, 1995

People may be starving around the world, but that's no excuse for the Lord to ignore those who've got plenty to eat. Like ribs.

When the coauthors of *The Ultimate Barbecue Sauce Cookbook* approached Big Daddy for his recipe, he chose to keep his kitchen secrets between himself and the Master Chef Upstairs. "It's kind of hard for me to talk about," he said, after explaining the divine inspiration.

Dismayed, the authors scurried about their kitchen trying to match the holy flavor and came very close but could not match the consistency. "I was sick of it and decided to just leave it out of the book," one of the authors said. "So I took the pot of sauce, put it in my sink and turned on the faucet to rinse it out." Suddenly, they had their answer—Big Daddy's last secret ingredient was one of God's originals: water.

GOD ISN'T MY COPILOT

"He told a flight attendant that God had ordered him to remain standing during landing."

Associated Press, reporting on Dean, a passenger who refused to sit down and threw the flight attendant over two rows of seats, 1999

In the pre-9/11 era, the unruly twenty-two-year-old hadn't been considered a threat as he roamed the aisles claiming to be Jesus, blessing passengers and touching the breasts of two other flight attendants. But when Dean was asked to take his seat, his sky rage erupted as he assaulted the offending crew member in order to uphold God's command. Four passengers managed to subdue him and constrain him using seat belts and an airline necktie.

Dean was sentenced to three years' probation and will never be given extra airline peanuts again.

"Breakfast Fit For A King"
JESUS
CONEY
ISLAND
BREAKFAST
&
HOT WINGS
OPEN 24 HOURS

HOLY NARCISSISM

"I had wanted [my restaurant] to be named after me. But God said it couldn't be like that."

Brymon, on why he was compelled to name his Memphis restaurant Jesus Coney Island, 2002

Brymon turned in his badge as a crime-fighting Detroit deputy sheriff in favor of moving south to sell hot wings, cheeseburgers, and grits. With God lending a mighty hand in naming the restaurant, patrons got their first taste of holy flavoring straight off the menu—a healthy dose of biblical quotes to balance out the unhealthy greasy goodness.

"So if they come in and just look at the menu and not buy anything, my job is done," Brymon explained. "This is not a restaurant; it's a ministry." And if they do buy something, how could Jesus not be a bit more popular when he comes with a side of fries?

THY NUDIST CLOWN CAR

"The Lord told them to get rid of all their belongings and go to Louisiana. So they got rid of all their clothes and pocketbooks and wallets and identification and the license plate off their car and came to our gorgeous state."

Police chief of Vinton, Louisiana, on the naked family of twenty he discovered after their car ran into a tree, 1993

When God told the family to get rid of everything, no one argued. Their 1990 Pontiac Grand Am, however, was spared as a means to drive from their native Floydada, Texas, to Louisiana. "They didn't have any money," the police chief said. "Not even a dime."

The accident occurred after an officer pulled the car over and a man emerged wearing only a towel, then jumped back in and sped off until the tree brought the vehicle back to a stop.

One by one, buck-naked passengers poured out, ranging in age from one to sixty-three.

"They were completely nude. All twenty of them. Didn't have a stitch of clothes on. I mean, no socks, no underwear, no nothin'. Five of them were in the trunk," the chief said.

On the bright side, they all served as human airbags, offering no room to get jerked around. Injuries were minor as a result.

The family claimed Satan was hot on their trail and Floydada would suffer total destruction if they stayed.

THE GOOD, THE BAD, AND THE DAMNATION

"God told him [Clint] Eastwood owed him money for three movies and would die by the end of April if he didn't pay."

Associated Press, reporting on the arrest of Brian, who harassed Eastwood for $5 million, 1992

The arrest came after Brian left a series of forty-three intimidating messages on Eastwood's production studio answering machine during the month of March. If Eastwood failed to pay by April 11, Brian said he would be dead within two weeks. Just for good measure, he also threatened the actor's two children.

Authorities had little trouble tracking down Dirty Harry's harasser, as he left his home phone number and address in several messages.

Brian told the FBI he never planned to harm the actor—that would be handled by God Himself. To date, He has yet to make Eastwood's day.

SOLE SAVIOR

"God told me to open up a shoe repair shop in the bus."

Don, on the Lord's entrepreneurial advice after fleeing to North Carolina from Colorado in a 1951 Studebaker bus, 1989

A fiery explosion at his church left Don with minor burns, major nerves, and an urgency to get out of town. "God said, 'Are you going to linger like Lot?' and I knew God was involved," he explained—although no reason for God's involvement in the blast was offered.

Don, a former Orthodox Jew who determined Jesus was in fact the Messiah, packed up his family and belongings and headed East with no idea of what he would do there. Fortunately, God came through with a plan. For $400, Don purchased the necessary shoe repair equipment and set up shop in his bus on the side of a North Carolina road.

After several years in the roadside cobbler business, Don expanded his enterprise under a more traditional roof, offering such additional services as VHS and cassette duplication, typesetting, and more. The new, improved shop found success and allowed Don to develop his personal global outreach ministry. "Our profit is used to buy mostly Bibles and things of that nature," he said. One thousand of those bibles were personally distributed across Nigeria. "We're kind of unique because of what we do and how we do it."

MORTGAGE BREAKER

"It was our desire to be free from this mortgage debt. Therefore we asked God our Heavenly Father...He heard us and He freed us from this mortgage bondage."

Norman and Melissa, on why they refused to pay back their $54,000 home loan from Fannie Mae, 1999

Before it had a mortgage-lending crisis to contend with, Fannie Mae found itself battling with divine intervention.

Norman and Melissa sought help from above after falling three months behind in their payments. God allegedly heard their prayers and gave them permission to stop payments altogether. Fannie Mae responded with an invitation to court, accompanied by a threat to take possession of the home.

In their defense, the couple filed court documents claiming they signed the mortgage "without being equipped with truth...and without Godly wisdom."

No doubt the Lord has been bombarded with similar requests in recent years.

FAITH AND FINANCES

"God spoke to me and said, 'Chuck, if you pastor the bank, I'll take care of the bottom line.'"

Chuck, cofounder of Riverview Community Bank, on plans to create a Christian international bank holding company, 2006

Finding early success with his Christian-based bank, Chuck planned to expand his financial proselytizing mission. As part of the bank's religious practices, Chuck prayed over customers, fusing faith with finance, and kept track of his converts.

But the bank's initial triumphs soon turned sour and expansion would no longer be an option. In 2009, federal regulators targeted the six-year-old Minnesota bank for making bad housing loans and executing "unsafe or unsound banking practices."

If a bank with God on its side couldn't avoid housing loan issues and losses galore, how could so many other banks across the nation have been expected to?

Whiteytown

ORDAINED HELLRAISER

"God told him to go to a white neighborhood and cause trouble."

Police sergeant, on why Aundre stole hot dogs and led cops on a bizarre car chase, 2001

Upon entering a "white" neighborhood, Aundre could have wreaked the Lord's havoc in any number of damaging ways. Fortunately, he chose a relatively innocuous form of trouble—he pilfered hotdogs (but not a single condiment) from a local grocery store. The mischief continued in the parking lot as twelve cruisers from four police departments pursued the hungry thief. A well-placed stop stick punctured one of Aundre's tires, causing him to hit a police vehicle and finally come to a stop. With his car out of commission, he surrendered to the law but did so knowing God's will was fulfilled.

PRAY THE STINK AWAY

"Two children and their mother lived for about two months with the decaying body of a 90-year-old woman on the toilet of their home's only bathroom...God told the mother she would come to life if she prayed hard enough."

Article reporting on Tammy, who kept the dead body on the toilet at the advice of her religious "superior," 2008

All the hard praying in the world couldn't bring the decomposing body back to life. It couldn't even stop the corpse from stinking up the entire house. Neither could Lysol.

Tammy's friend, a self-described bishop, directed her to leave the dead body propped up on the toilet because God said He would eventually whip up a miraculous resurrection. The children were told that sneaky demons were responsible for the decay so it would look like the old lady may not return to life.

In the meantime, the family used a makeshift toilet elsewhere in the house. It, too, failed to mask the smell of the carcass.

The body was finally discovered when a deputy knocked

on the door, visiting at the request of the elderly woman's sister who hadn't heard from her in an unusually long time. Tammy informed her that Grandma had gone on vacation, but the horrid stench crept through the door and the officer caught a whiff.

The deputy followed her nose to the toilet and discovered the lump that was left of the woman. The children were ordered out of the home and into foster care. Tammy and her religious advisor were charged with causing mental harm to a child and obstructing justice.

GOD CREATED THE SEAS AND SAW IT WAS GOOD FOR SWIMMING

"The voice of the Lord told me I should swim the English Channel."

Reverend Richard, of Westcliff-on-Sea, England, on why he planned to attempt a feat far beyond his abilities, 1972

Richard was innocently walking home from church one night when God seemingly decided his evening stroll wasn't nearly enough exercise. Swimming the English Channel, however, would do the trick.

The forty-seven-year-old reverend had never swum more than three miles but was determined to heed God's order and make the twenty-two-mile trek within six weeks. "When the Lord gives a command, even to swim the channel, he also gives the strength to do it," Richard said. But just in case, he tried to supply himself with his own added strength by training seventy-two hours a week, including a daily dip in the sea each morning.

No reports offered any news of his success or failure.

HEIST GLORY

"The Lord specifically commanded me to rob the banks so that's what I did."

James, testifying in his defense after committing the largest bank robbery in Los Angeles history, 1993

According to the forty-nine-year-old thief, God not only guided him into bank robbery superstardom, but He even advised him to use gloves and disguises. In all, James and his codefendant, Gilbert, hauled off nearly $1 million in nine robberies—including a record $430,000 from one bank—before being captured by the FBI.

Taking God's advice, James robbed banks wearing latex gloves, various disguises (with occasional fake mustaches), and made use of multiple getaway cars.

The robberies were arranged to help Gilbert recover money he and James believed was taken as part of a massive banking and candymaker conspiracy. Gilbert had been in the fudge-making business, and the two men thought a jealous competitor and evil banks wanted to destroy his venture. James felt he was simply repossessing Gilbert's money, not stealing it. Plus, "the Lord commissioned me," he testified.

Yet, the money was not put into producing a million dollars' worth of delicious fudge but was used instead to buy guns, bullets, cars, and motorcycles. The FBI uncovered an armory of 119 guns and more than 27,000 rounds of ammunition in the duo's lavish rented home—which featured a bunker and shooting range beneath it. James and Gilbert explained that they were gearing up for Armageddon.

Unfortunately, with a sentence of thirty years in prison, James would have to face Armageddon with no arms but the ones God gave him. Gilbert was found not guilty by reason of insanity.

60
55
50
Holy Bible

MERRY MISDEMEANOR

"We've seen nuns and priests in here telling us that God told them to [shoplift]."

Tammy, store security officer, describing the variety of shoplifters caught during the holiday season, 1993

During a time when voracious shoppers are trampled to death while seeking bargains and must-have items, God really should be helping, not hurting, the stores. Let's just hope that unlike the college kid Tammy caught, the nuns and priests weren't stealing condoms.

FALLEN FURTHER FROM GRACE

"God told me to [ban Satan from my town]."

Carolyn, mayor of the small town of Inglis, Florida, on her official proclamation forbidding the devil entry into the city limits, 2002

God's help in banishing that evil Lucifer from town is actually a wonderful deed befitting of a morally perfect deity. Residents should feel a sense of peace knowing that the devil isn't welcome and that the Lord Himself is ready to enforce the proclamation. But what about residents outside of town? If God is going to ban Satan, He really shouldn't play favorites with Inglis; He should ban that damn demon from every town, village, city, state, desert, mountain, small island, houseboat, and any other place evil can show its filthy face.

As for Inglis (population 1,400), the mayor took God's word and ran with it. The Almighty even guided her hand in writing the official proclamation, which read:

> Be it known from this day forward that Satan, ruler of darkness, giver of evil, destroyer of what is good and just, is not now, nor ever again will be, a part of this town of Inglis. Satan is hereby declared powerless, no longer ruling over, nor influencing, our citizens...We exercise our authority over the devil in Jesus' name. By that authority, and through His Blessed Name, we command all Satanic and demonic forces to cease their activities and depart the town of Inglis.

The document was signed by the town clerk, stamped with the official seal, and posted around Inglis.

"People call and ask me, 'Carolyn, is Satan there?' And I tell them, 'Satan is only where we let him,'" the mayor said. "I did what was best for my town and my people."

Now, the only thing officially being damned in the small town is the separation of church and state.

PARTING WORDS

Are you there God? It's me, Marc.

Within moments, a small twig lying on the ground near me began to spark with a flame and God spoketh these words:

GOD: *You have finished the book. Hallelujah. But there are many other things I have said that I did not see in these pages. What about all the things I said to Joan? They burned her for it!*

MH: *Joan?*

GOD: *Of Arc. French kid, got sainted.*

MH: *I thought I'd keep things a bit more modern, you know? Besides, the publisher only gave me 288 pages, and that includes the bibliography. Good Lord, what do you want from me?*

GOD: *Yet, you waste a perfectly good page reprinting this conversation?*

MH: *You knew I was writing this page before it was published and you said nothing. You stayed silent. Grant me a sequel and I will print more. Now, go help those in need. Answer zillions of prayers. Watch football. Tell someone to chop off a hand. Go damn something!*

GOD: *Amen.*

PHOTO CREDITS

"Unheavenly Home," "Busker Miracles," "Blind Attack," "No Daily Bread" (bowl and background), "The Gift of Snacking," "OMG, WTF God?" "Blessed Bribery" photos © Liz Steger, lizsteger.com: 10, 12, 80, 90, 92, 128, 184; "Exalted Pickup" photo © Tammy Cromer-Campbell: 106; "White House of the Lord" courtesy of Sam J. Steger: 68; "Bible Mobile" (Lynn Gandy, "Jesus Truck"), "Cross Walk" (Lance Rowe, "Walking Jesus"), photos © Harrod Blank, www.harrodblank.com: 130, 146; "Holy Narcissism," photo © Theresa M. Zelasko: 234; all other photos are stock.

BIBILIOGRAPHY

TRAFFIC ENLIGHTENMENT

"Topless woman directs traffic in DeLand." News-JournalOnline.com, April 18, 2008, http://www.news-journalonline.com/special/dumbcrime/nakedtraffic041808.htm (accessed August 27, 2008).

ZOMBIE PRAYERS

Associated Press. "Couple Told to Bury Daughter Despite Belief." *Syracuse Herald-Journal*, September 23, 1983.

Associated Press. "Minister: Postponement Wrong." *Aiken (SC) Standard*, September 28, 1983.

United Press International. "Couple Ordered to Bury Child Dead 10 Weeks." *(Logansport, IN) Pharos-Tribune*, September 20, 1983.

AN OFFICER AND A DEITY

"Man Is Charged with Mischief for Hitting Patrol Car." *Everett (WA) Daily Herald*, April 28, 2006.

UNHEAVENLY HOME

Associated Press. "Killer of Slovenly Wife to get Chair." *Washington Post*, January 15, 1933.

BUSKER MIRACLES

Thompson, Jamie. "Juggler Says, 'God Told Me to Come.'" *St. Petersburg Times Online*, March 31, 2005, http://www.sptimes.com/2005/03/31/Tampabay/Juggler_says___God_to.shtml (accessed August 1, 2008).

WORDS FROM WAY ABOVE

Staff Reports. "Oral Roberts Tells of Talking to 900-Foot Jesus." Tulsaworld.com, October 16, 1980.

NEAR-DEATH EXPERIENCE

Briggs, David. "Oral History: Minister Follows Voice of God." *Frederick (MD) News-Post*, July 8, 1995.

PROFESSIONAL APOCALYPSE

Associated Press. "President of Oral Roberts University Resigns." November 23, 2007, http://wcbstv.com/national/OralRoberts.president.resigns.2.594512.html (accessed October 13, 2008).

SERPENT'S SANCTUARY

Associated Press. "For Snake Handler's Orphans, Custody Battle Pits Faith vs. Well-being." *Chillicothe Constitution-Tribune*, December 7, 1998.

"Custody of 'Snake-Bite Orphans' Split between Grandparents." CNN.com, February 12, 1999, http://www.cnn.com/US/9902/12/snake.bite.family/index.html (accessed June 26, 2009).

30,000 MILES CLOSER TO GOD

BBC World News America. "God Told Me to Buy a Citation 10." www.youtube.com/watch?v=bkWp75uQjWw (accessed November 28, 2008).

Keteyian, Armen. "Hard Questions for 'Prosperity Gospel.'" CBSNews.com, January 29, 2008.

OUR FATHER, OUR DINNER

Associated Press. "God Told Us to Eat Plane Crash Victim: Survivor." *Los Angeles Times*, June 1, 1979.

HOLY ART THOU, HERMIT

"Hermit Brings a Message." *New York Times*, August 11, 1911.

7TH-INNING SALVATION

Dart, John. "Miracles an Everyday Event to the Pentecostals." *Los Angeles Times*, January 11, 1976.

CLEANSE THY DRUG MONEY

Associated Press. "Accused Money-Laundering Pastor's Trial to Begin." *Victoria Advocate*, December 18, 1995.

"Preacher Seen on Videotape in Money Laundering Scheme." *(New Braunfels and Comal County, TX) Herald-Zeltung*, December 19, 1995.

Rodriguez, Joe. "Brace to Stand Trial of State Fraud Charges." *Wichita Eagle*, December 2, 1997.

TOILET PAPER TABERNACLE

Doto, Pamela. "Police Station Vandal Says God Told Him To Do It; 'Jesus' Toilet-Papers Trees." *Anchorage Daily News*, September 23, 1993.

HIGHER POWER HORSEPOWER

Associated Press. "Woman Who Claimed God Sent Her Gets Jail Time." May 18, 2004.

FATHER'S FULL MONTY

Baldwin, Paul. "Thongs of Praise! God Told Me to Become Saucy Male Stripper; My Act's Not a Sin, Says Sacked RE Teacher Robert." *The People (London)*, July 5, 1998.

HALLOWED HOOKER

"American Notes Scandals." *Time*, October 28, 1991.

Associated Press. "Swaggart Returns to Pulpit: God Told Him Not to Quit, Evangelist Says." *(Fredericksburg, VA) Free-Lance Star*, October 17, 1991.

FALSE PROPHECY

"Robertson: God 'will remove judges from the Supreme Court quickly'." Mediamatters.org, January 4, 2005, http://mediamatters.org/research/200501040010 (accessed September 18, 2008).

OMNIFICKLE

Associated Press. "'God Changed His Mind'; Mountaineer Still Lives." *Albuquerque Journal*, June 30, 1958.

PETROL PRAYERS ANSWERED

"Faith Healer Fills Teeth...Gas Tank, Too." *Chicago Tribune*, September 22, 1982.

LAZARUS, ESQ.

"Dug Up Casket During Night." *Boston Daily Globe*, February 4, 1911.

FAITH BLINDS

"He'd Let Snake Bite Again." *Washington Post*, August 15, 1934.

BABEL BABBLE

Bailey, Marie R. "Their Wits Are Awry." *Washington Post*, November 8, 1894.

SPANK THY LOVED ONES

Reeger, Jennifer. "New Ken Paddle Maker up against National Battle." *Pittsburgh Tribune-Review*, July 25, 2007.

HAVE FAITH IN VIOLENCE

The Way of the Master Radio. "Todd Bentley's Violent 'Ministry.'" www.youtube.com/watch?v=yN9Ay4QAtW8&feature=channel (accessed August 6, 2008).

DON KING OF ALL KINGS

Berkow, Ira. "A Sluggish Pursuit, Mostly by Faith." *New York Times*, January 7, 2005.

Juipe, Dean. "Evander Makes Prediction: Third-Round KO." *Las Vegas Sun*, February 25, 1999.

LEND ME THY HAND

Associated Press. "Man Recovers from Hand Amputation." *Albuquerque Tribune*, November 2, 1971.

LEND ME THY ENTIRE ARM

"Thrusts Arm Under Wheel." *Washington Post*, January 3, 1913.

SURGICAL COMMANDMENT

"Man Critically Wounded Allegedly by Own Act." *Hartford Courant*, January 17, 1949.

ALMIGHTY COMMANDER IN CHIEF

MacAskill, Ewen. "George Bush: 'God Told Me to End the Tyranny in Iraq'; President told Palestinians God Also Talked to Him about Middle East Peace." *The Guardian (UK)*, October 7, 2005, http://www.guardian.co.uk/world/2005/oct/07/iraq.usa (accessed July 28, 2008).

UNGODLY MESS

Beam, Christopher. "The Zeitgeist Checklist." *Washington Post*, January 5, 2007.

Obama, Barack. "A New Beginning." Speech Given at Cairo University, June 4, 2009, http://www.whitehouse.gov/the_press_office/Remarks-by-the-President-at-Cairo-University-6-04-09/ (accessed June 22, 2009).

Statistics cited: http://usliberals.about.com/od/homelandsecurit1/a/IraqNumbers.htm.

RUNNING ON A PRAYER

"Huckabee: Divine Providence Helps My Poll Numbers." http://www.youtube.com/watch?v=NSQNSlUUoOc (accessed November 22, 2008).

THE PERILOUS HIGHWAY TO HEAVEN

Degette, Cara. "Duke Fingers Hefleys in Conspiracy." *Colorado Springs Independent* Online Edition, April 13, 2000, http://www.csindy.com/gyrobase/Content?oid=oid%3A1394 (accessed September 22, 2008).

X-RATED VISION

Braver, Rita. "Interview with Pat Robertson, Part 1." *CBS News Sunday Morning,* April 9, 2006, http://www.cbsnews.com/stories/2006/04/07/sunday/main1481775.shtml (accessed September 24, 2008).

MONOCONSTITUENTISM

Bachmann, Michele. "'God Called Me to Run for Congress." http://www.youtube.com/watch?v=l0rUBomKvY0 (accessed November 16, 2008).

SODOM AND LOS ANGELES

"Congregation Moves to Missouri: Group Fears California Doomed." *(Jefferson City, MO) Daily Capital News*, February 21, 1969.

ELECTION INTERVENTION

Carlson, Peter. "More Than You Wanted to Know about the Election." *(Bergen County, NJ), The Record* cited in *Washington Post*. October 31, 2004.

OUR FIRST LADY OF NO MERCY

Polley, Gerald. "An Open Letter To First Lady Laura Bush From

Speaker Gerald Polley, God's Candidate For The Presidency." http://www.voicesfromspirit.com/geraldtolaurabush.htm (accessed November 11, 2008).
Skelton, Kathryn. "Weird, Wicked Weird: Lewiston-born Gerald Polley Tried to Run for President with First Lady Laura Bush as Veep. It Didn't Work, but He's pressing On." *(Lewiston, ME) Sun Journal,* November 11, 2008.

WHITE HOUSE OF THE LORD

Smith, Tristan. "Tough Sell at White House of Atlanta." CNN.com, January 28, 2009.

BLESSED ARE THE MINNESOTA VIKINGS

Dufresne, Chris. "Does God Care Who Wins?" *Los Angeles Times,* February 21, 1999.

TRAILER CRASH

"Crashes Trailers to get People Up for Church." *Hartford Courant,* March 11, 1963.

HUNGER SAVES?

"Too Busy With Store to Join the Church." *Boston Globe,* January 10, 1921.

HUNGER DOTH NOT SAVE

Associated Press. "Illinois Man Dies in 104th Day of Fast." *Pittsburgh Post-Gazette,* July 22, 1949.
Associated Press. "Self-Imposed Fast Kills Man." *St. Petersburg Times,* July 22, 1949.

CURVEBALL FROM ABOVE

Edes, Gordon. "'God's Orders' Send Pitcher Packing." *Chicago Tribune,* June 30, 1978.

HIGH WIRE TO HEAVEN

Associated Press. "Karl Wallenda Is Buried in Sarasota, FL, Beside 3 Other Family High-Wire Victims." *New York Times*, March 28, 1978.

SPIRITUAL SHOPLIFTING

"In the Name of God." *Los Angeles Times*, September 20, 1913.

BLIND ATTACK

Christmas, Faith C. "Man Tries to 'Cure' Singer's Blindness." *Los Angeles Sentinel*, March 3, 1977.

THOU SHALT STIFF THY WAITRESS

Mailer, Norman, with Michael Lennon. *On God: An Uncommon Conversation*. New York: Random House, 2007.

BEYOND CIRCUMCISION

Associated Press. "'God Told Me To Do It,' Says Mill Worker Who Performed Crude Operation on Brother." *Amarillo Sunday News and Globe*, December 22, 1935.

GOD'S REPUBLICAN

McKeon, Albert. "For a Mere $1,000, Anyone Can...Aspire to Greatness." NashuaTelegraph.com, December 9, 2007.

SPREAD MY WORD AND THY CASH

Associated Press. "Fantastic Case Solved; Culprit Goes to Asylum." *Pacific Stars & Stripes*, July 29, 1951.

SANTA LUCIFER

"So They Say." *Manitowac Herald-Times*, December 20, 1961.

NO DAILY BREAD

Associated Press. "Fasts 36 Days 'At Lord's Call.'" *Jefferson City Post Tribune*, April 15, 1937.

Associated Press. "Mountain Faster Growing Stronger; Says Lord Prescribed Squirrel Soup." *Albuquerque Journal*, May 2, 1937.

"Religion: In Stooping Oak." *Time*, May 10, 1937, http://www.time.com/time/magazine/article/0,9171,757781,00.html (accessed August 9, 2009).

THE GIFT OF SNACKING

"Bill Mallory: Steps of Faith." Newsletter, Point Loma Nazarene University, May 2008, http://www.pointloma.edu/Alumni/Alumni Publications/eNews/eNewsarchive/May2008Newsletter.htm (accessed September 23, 2008).

MOTOR CITY SAMSON

Associated Press. "Nomad, Wife Live Three Years in Car." *Hartford Courant*, February 28, 1966.

WANDERING AIMLESSLY IN THE DESERT

Boivin, Paola. "Cards Optimism is Back; Dare We Hop on Bandwagon?" *Arizona Republic*, August 30, 2007.

ROADSIDE BENEDICTION

DeSmet, Kate. "Texan Toasts His Prayer Walk and Leaves Miracles to God." *Chicago Tribune*, February 17, 1983.

LUMBERJESUS

Ransom, Franki V. "A Life-size Toothpick Jesus—`God Told Me To Do It.'" *Chicago Sun-Times*, August 28, 1991.

THE PARTING OF THE PUDDLES

"Says Lord Kept Her Feet Dry." *New York Tribune*, September 18, 1903.

SEEKERS OF THE LOST ARK

Sun-Times Wires. "Ex-Astronaut: God Told Me to Find Ark." *Chicago Sun-Times*, August 29, 1986.

LESBIAN SEX SHALL BE FORBIDDEN IN THE LIBRARY

Prudenti, Richard Dean, "Man Threatens Legal Action Against City Bentonville Resident Unhappy Because Of Sex Guide Book." *(Northwest Arkansas) Morning News*, April 19, 2007, http://www.nwaonline.net/articles/2007/04/19/news/042007bzsuterfolo.txt (accessed September 4, 2008).

EXALTED PICKUP

Hands on a Hard Body. Directed by Bindler, S. R. Idea Entertainment, 1998.

THE LORD'S LOOPHOLE

"Man Says God Told Him Not to Pay Income Tax." *Los Angeles Times*, July 1, 1979.

THE BIG WHEEL IN THE SKY

Ray, Julie. "Price is right for Nellis Airman." *Airman's World*, September 1, 2004.

THE END WAS NEAR

"Ugandan Cult Member's Warning." *BBC News*, March 20, 2000.

THE UGANDAN MOSES

"Uganda Arrests Doomsday Cult Leaders." *Conspiracy Times*, September 26, 2007.

THE KING DETHRONES THE EMPEROR

"Ex-Kaiser Says God May Call Him Back." *New York Times*, October 10, 1927.

THOU SHALT HIT OVER AND OVER AND OVER AGAIN

http://www.crimezzz.net/serialkillers/C/CARIGNAN_harvey_louis.php (accessed September 2, 2008).

http://www.serialkillerdatabase.net/harveycarignan.html (accessed September 2, 2008).

AND YE SHALL FEAST ON HER FLESH

Dean, Kenneth. "Cannibalism Suspect: 'God Told Me To Do It.'" *Tyler (TX) Morning Telegraph*, January 7, 2008.

CRUCIFIXATION

Hines, Nico. "'God Made Me Cancel My Own Crucifixion.'" *The Times (UK)*, April 15, 2006. http://www.timesonline.co.uk/tol/news/world/asia/article705815.ece (accessed October 10, 2008).

CONTEMPT FOR COURT

Associated Press. "4 Minn. Men Sentenced in Threatened-Judge Case." wcco.com, February 23, 2009, http://wcco.com/crime/threatened.judge.sentencing.2.942234.html (accessed June 20, 2009).

Tevlin, Jon. "God Wants Me to Destroy the Judge." Startribune.com, July 16, 2008, http://www.startribune.com/local/25539759.html?location_refer=Homepage:latestNews:4 (accessed September 15, 2008).

DEMONS WITHIN AND AROUND

Associated Press. "Crippled Youth is Starved to Death." *(Moberly, MO) Monitor-Index and Democrat*, June 17, 1932.

BEHOLD AND BEHEAD

Hopkins, Kathleen. "Murder Suspect Testifies God Ordered Him to Kill." *Asbury Park Press*, August 26, 2008.

"NJ Man Who Says God Told Him to Kill is Convicted." MyCentralJersey.com, September 2, 2008.

HOLY WAR OF THE WORLDS

Shriner, Sherry. *Bible Codes Revealed: The Coming UFO Invasion.* iUniverse, Inc., 2005.

GRAND PRIX-CHER

Chaytor, Rod. "I Felt God Was by My Side: Madcap Priest Who Dodged F1 Cars Walks Free." *(London, England) The Mirror,* September 2, 2003.

Foley, Cliona. "Defrocked Priest Says He's Sorry and Walks Free." *Europe Intelligence Wire,* August 31, 2004.

OMG, WTF GOD?

Lundbacck, Karin. "Tale of Sex, Murder, God and SMS Grips Sweden." *Free Press Of Namibia,* June 11, 2004.

BIBLE MOBILE

Blank, Harrod. *Wild Wheels.* Documentary, Harrod Blank Creations, 1992.

CHURCHYARD SHELTER

Associated Press. "Church Congregation Must Decide Whether to Oust Yearlong Squatter." *Chillicothe Constitution-Tribune,* May 20, 1996.

OMNIPRESENT WITNESS

Associated Press. "Tips Came from Many Sources." *Jefferson City (MO) Post Tribune,* December 8, 1977.

REALITY SHOW INTERVENTION

"Suspicion Grows about America's Player; Amber Says God Told Her She'd Be in the Final Two." Realityblurred.com, August 20, 2007, http://www.realityblurred.com/realitytv/archives/big_brother_8/2007_Aug_20_suspicion_grows (accessed October 18, 2008).

30-FOOT LEAP OF FAITH

McPhee, Michele, and Alice McQuillan. "Man Leaps—And Lives. Air Bag Cushions 30-Ft. Fall." *New York Daily News*, January 6, 1997.

JUDAS GOES TO COURT

"'God Told Me to Testify against OJ.'" Metro.co.uk. September 25, 2008, http://www.metro.mobi/article/326306/i/2 (accessed October 25, 2008).

KING SOLOMON OF SUSSEX

Pettifor, Tom. "The Man with Seven Wives: God Told Me to Live like King, Says Furniture Salesman." *(Glasgow, Scotland) Daily Record*, April 20, 2006.

UNDRESSED TO KILL

Harrell, Jeff. "Driver's Demeanor after Running Down Attorney under Scrutiny." *Staten Island Advance*, October 17, 2008.

STREET SOVEREIGN

"Driving Charge Preacher's Direct Line to God." *(Glasgow, Scotland) Daily Record*, April 18, 2001.

SUPREME PUPPET MASTER

Maheras, Nick G. "Traveler Spreads His Message across the Nation." *High Point (NC) Enterprise*, January 8, 2007.

WANDERING TO AND FRO

Patrick, Nikki. "Walking for God." *Pittsburg (KS) Morning Sun*, August 25, 2008.

MODERN-DAY METHUSELAH

Coughlan, Artemis. "'The Urinator' Hit with 43; Will Be 20,043 at Release." *(Trenton, NJ) Trentonian*, July 18, 2008.

CROSS WALK

http://crosscountry4jesus.com/ (accessed January 15, 2009).

Rhodes, Steve. "Family in Bus Follows Their Lord across Hills and Valleys of America." *(Cedar Valley, IA) Waterloo Courier,* December 25, 1991.

HE MADE THE MAID DO IT

"Crazed by Religion, Maid with Axe Kills One and Gashes Two." *New York Times,* November 28, 1924.

UNREAL ESTATE

"An Ad and a Prayer: Vineland Pastor Advertises for Benefactor." *Press of Atlantic City (NJ),* January 14, 2002.

DIVINE CHEESEHEAD

Krattenmaker, Tom. "Reggie's (Whole) Story." *USA Today,* August 3, 2006.

ALMIGHTY BED

"Nigerian Faces Death for 86 Wives." *BBC News,* August 21, 2008.

Walker, Andrew. "Nigerian Advises against 86 Wives." *BBC News,* August 8, 2008

RECKLESS SPIRITUAL JOURNEY

Barrett, Robertson. "Clues to Why Driver Let Bus Drag Car Scare." *News & Observer (NC),* November 14, 1991.

THE PASSING OF WIND

King, Peter. "Inside the NFL: Divine Intervention." *Sports Illustrated,* October 21, 1998.

ORIGINAL MATCHMAKER

Hockaday, Sabrina. "Teacher's Proposal Bugs Student." *Long Beach (CA) Press-Telegram*, June 18, 1992.

HOLY SHIT

UPI NewsTrack. "Outreach Minister Finds Mission in Dog Doo." April 7, 2006.

DOGGY HEAVEN ON EARTH

Chapman, Dan. "Court May Tally Dog's Life Tab." *Atlanta Journal-Constitution*, June 1, 2003.

JOSEPH AND THE BUDGET OF MANY DOLLARS

"'Audience of One' Tracks One Man's Movie Quest." National Public Radio, *Weekend Edition*, Saturday, March 17, 2007, http://www.npr.org/templates/transcript/transcript.php?storyId=8972583 (accessed November 11, 2008).

http://www.zoominfo.com/people/Gazowsky_Richard_34270642.aspx (accessed November 11, 2008).

ROAD WRATH

McClure, Sue. "Shots Halt Big Rig's Charge in Columbia." *Tennessean*, October 6, 2001.

HOCKING HOLY MATRIMONY

"Best Combination Pawnshop and Wedding Chapel." Houston-Press.com, 2001.

Isay, Dave (Producer) and Jude Doherty (Editor). "Kipperman's Pawnshop." National Public Radio, *All Things Considered*, February 12, 1993.

THOU SHALT ALMOST WIN

"The Bubba Paris Story." *Answer: Business Men's Fellowship International,* Vol. IV, No. 1, pages 6–9.

SUPREME OOPS

"'God Told Me To Kill'; Declares Insane Slayer." *Atlanta Daily World,* February 23, 1937.

TRUCK STOPPER

Kennedy, Dana. "Family Crisscrosses U.S. Taking Jesus to Truckers." *Los Angeles Times,* February 10, 1983.

YEE HAW-LLELUJAH

Wilson, Cathy. "Cowboy Church: They're Not just Horsing Around." *Perquimans Weekly,* June 3, 2009.

GOD FRAUD

Harris, Art. "Jim Bakker: 'I Was Doing My Best'." *Washington Post,* September 30, 1989.

News Services. "Top PTL Aide Pleads Guilty to Fraud." *Washington Post,* August 9, 1989.

LET THERE BE MILLIONS

Kindred, Dave. "1997 Ad." *The Sporting News,* December 29, 1997, http://findarticles.com/p/articles/mi_m1208/is_n52_v221/ai_20208897/?tag=content;col1 (accessed December 19, 2008).

Kindred, Dave. "In the name of sanity." *The Sporting News,* April 20, 1998, http://findarticles.com/p/articles/mi_m1208/is_n16_v222/ai_n27523733/ (accessed December 19, 2008).

BIG BANG II

Associated Press. "Detroit Man Dies Dynamiting Hotel; Five Hurt." *Albuquerque Tribune,* May 1, 1954.

RETURNS MESSIAH

"10 Tax Preparers Accused of Frauds." *New York Times*, January 17, 1973.

MOTHER MARY JANE

"Creator Told Me to Grow Pot, Man Tells Trial." *CBC News*, February 6, 2008.

Pacholik, Barb. "Agecoutay Appeals Trafficking Sentence." *(Canada) Leader-Post*, May 2, 2008.

LORD 1, LANDLORD 0

Lii, Jane H. "Debtor's Dogs, Landlord's Headache." *New York Times*, December 12, 1997.

BLESSED BRIBERY

Rhoades, Todd. "Paying People to Attend Church Plan Fails." *Dallas Morning News*, September 23, 2004.

THE WRITING ON THE SKY

Associated Press. "God Writers in the Sky." January 4, 2002, http://www.skeptictank.org/gen4/gen02335.htm (accessed November 20, 2008).

Kaye, Ken. "Florida Skywriter to Show Off Aerial Penmanship at Air & Sea Show." *South Florida Sun-Sentinel*, April 19, 2007.

DEAR LORD

"Even 'Right' Behavior Can Sometimes Be Wrong." *St. Petersburg Times*, August 12, 1980.

BROKEN PROMISES

"She Awaits Death." *Washington Post*, June 14, 1908.

UNTAKEN SACRED VOWS

"Directed Here in a Vision." *Washington Post*, October 6, 1906.

SOYLENT GOD

Zahir, Fazile. "A Meaty Tale of Sordid Murder." *Asia Times Online*, October 3, 2007, http://www.atimes.com/atimes/middle_east/ij03ak01.html (accessed January 10, 2009).

INFERNAL AFFAIR

Bartley, Nancy and Dee Norton. "Officer Thwarts Fire at Church; Woman Arrested." *Seattle Times*, August 10, 1996.

NO RAM THIS TIME

"Alexandrian Kills Mother as She Views Movie on TV." *Washington Post and Times Herald*, September 27, 1956.

"'God Told Me', Son Says of TV Killing." *Washington Post and Times Herald*, September 28, 1956.

BAD LUCK CAT

"Albert Houston Committed to Mental Health Facility." *Syracuse Herald-Journal*, October 19, 1985.

Hedglon, Mary. "Slaying Case: A Quiet Couple." *Syracuse Herald-Journal*, October 9, 1984.

RIGHTEOUS ROAD TRIP

Associated Press. "Speeder Pays Fine Unasked." *Washington Post and Times Herald*, June 15, 1962.

BAD BEGETS EVIL

Associated Press. "Held in Slaying." *Washington Post*, December 19, 1962.

LACK OF JUDGMENT DAY

United Press International. "God told me to leave Princeton." *(Elyria, OH) Chronicle-Telegram*, June 8, 1982.

MESSIAH LIBIDO

Pereira, Jen, Kiran Khalid, and Stephanie Dahle. "Teens Taken from Cult at Center of New Film." ABCNews.com, May 2, 2008.

Shiflett, Dave. "Wacky Cult Leader Beds Naked Virgins, Son's Wife." *Bloomberg News*, May 5, 2008.

NOAH JR.

Hyer, Marjorie. "Maryland Pastor Building an Ark." *Washington Post*, November 7, 1977.

NOAH III

Tomb, Geoffrey. "Ark Taking Shape for Mission to Haiti." *Miami Herald*, November 13, 1994.

BLOW WORSHIP

LaFraniere, Sharon. "Barry Arrested on Cocaine Charges in Undercover FBI, Police Operation. Sources Say Mayor Used Crack in Downtown D.C. Hotel Room." *Washington Post*, January 19, 1990.

Leff, Lisa. "Barry Says He 'Will Rise Again' after Trial." *Washington Post*, July 16, 1990.

EXODUS FROM THE LAND OF FLORIDA

Associated Press. "Tidal Wave? Woman's 'Vision' Prompts an Exodus to the Hills." *(St. Petersburg, FL) Evening Independent*, April 2, 1976.

United Press International. "Latins Flee Miami, Fearful of Prophecy." *St. Petersburg Times*, April 3, 1976.

THOU SHALT GET FREAKY

"Christian Pair's Sex Shop Website." *BBC News*, April 13, 2006.

HOLY MOLE MEN

"America Hasn't Been Destroyed by A-bombs and Full Gospel Assembly Is Losing Patience." *Los Angeles Times*, February 11, 1970.

Associated Press. "Two Members of Religious Sect Arrested." *Kingsport (TN) News*, July 11, 1960.

"Sealed-Up Sect." *Time*, August 8, 1960.

BLESSED AGORAPHOBIA, PART 1

Associated Press. "Sheriffs Drag Cultists from Conn. Motel." *Boston Globe*, October 6, 1983.

BLESSED AGORAPHOBIA, PART 2

Associated Press. "Police Evict 3 Cultists from Jail in Connecticut Town." *Boston Globe*, January 30, 1984.

PICKUP TAKEDOWN

Crowe, Robert. "Driver Said God Ordered 100-mph Wreck." *(San Antonio, TX) Express-News*, November 28, 2008.

THE DIVINE RIGHT TO BEAR ARMS

Darnell, Jim. "Belgium Browning Sweet Sixteen Still One of My Favorite Shotguns." *San Marcos (TX) Daily Record*, December 4, 2008.

DOOM AND PRISON GLOOM

Associated Press. "Family Predicts Town's Doom." *Bridgeport (KS) Telegram*, March 21, 1960.

Associated Press. "Kansas Family Split Up by Law." *(Jefferson City, MO) Post-Tribune*, March 22, 1962.

THE ROOFS ARE ON FIRE

United Press International. "Doukhobors Burn Up 53 of Their Homes." *Chicago Daily Tribune*, June 9, 1962.

"The Doukhobors." *Oakland Tribune*, February 2, 1954.

LOUIS THE APOSTLE

"Three Men Subdue a Lunatic." *New York Tribune*, December 23, 1900.

ADD A PINCH OF GOD

Sagon, Candy. "Barbecue Testers Hit the Sauce for Cookbook." *Pittsburgh Post-Gazette*, cited in *Washington Post*, August 23, 1995.

GOD ISN'T MY COPILOT

Associated Press. "Airline Passenger Guilty of 'Sky Rage.'" *Frederick (MD) Post*, January 13, 1999.

Associated Press. "Man Gets Probation for Assault on Plane." *(Annapolis, MD) Sunday Capital*, May 2, 1999.

HOLY NARCISSISM

Price, Stephen D. "Save Room for Salvation: At Jesus Coney Island, Heaven's a Hot Wing Away." *Memphis (TN) Commercial Appeal*, February 14, 2002.

THY NUDIST CLOWN CAR

Associated Press. "20 Naked People Emerge after Auto Strikes Tree; Texas Family Didn't Have `Even a Dime.'" *Washington Post*, August 20, 1993.

THE GOOD, THE BAD, AND THE DAMNATION

Associated Press. "'God' Says Eastwood Owes Man Money." *Indiana Gazette*, April 11, 1992.

SOLE SAVIOR

Fellers, Tracie. "God Spoke, And Don Kistler's Glad He Listened To Him 15 Years Ago." *Charlotte (NC) Observer*, January 21, 1989.

MORTGAGE BREAKER

Associated Press. "Pair says God freed them of mortgage." *Boston Globe,* August 11, 1999.

FAITH AND FINANCES

Serres, Chris. "Otsego Bank Cited for Unsound Practices." *(Minneapolis-St. Paul, MN) Star Tribune*, May 29, 2009.

ORDAINED HELLRAISER

Houck, Jeanne. "Suspect: God Told Him To Do It." *Cincinnati Post*, September 3, 2001.

PRAY THE STINK AWAY

Associated Press. "Kids, Mom Lived with 90-Year-Old's Corpse for Weeks in Wisconsin." FoxNews.com, May 9, 2008, http://www.foxnews.com/story/0,2933,354849,00.html (accessed December 10, 2008).

GOD CREATED THE SEAS AND SAW IT WAS GOOD FOR SWIMMING

"Believes Lord Will Aid Channel Swim." *Chicago Tribune*, June 22, 1972.

HEIST GLORY

Tamaki, Julie. "God Told Him to Rob Banks, Man Testifies Courts." *Los Angeles Times*, September 30, 1993.

MERRY MISDEMEANOR

Aitchison, Diana. "Store Detectives Braced for Holiday Rush." *St. Louis Post-Dispatch*, December 11, 1993.

FALLEN FURTHER FROM GRACE

Bragg, Rick. "Florida Town Finds Satan an Offense." *New York Times*, March 14, 2002.

ABOUT THE AUTHOR

"God told me to dig up his most dreadful and absurd advice and deliver it unto the masses."

Marc Hartzman, author, *God Made Me Do It*, on why he wrote this book, 2009

This is Hartzman's third book but the first directly commanded from the Lord above. His other books, *Found on eBay: 101 Genuinely Bizarre Items From the World's Online Yard Sale* (Universe/Rizzoli) and *American Sideshow: An Encyclopedia of History's Most Wondrous and Curiously Strange Performers* (Tarcher/Penguin), were written entirely without God's blessing; however, He was surely aware of both.

When not doing the Lord's work, Hartzman clings mightily to his soul while serving companies big and small as a writer in the advertising industry.